OCCASIONAL PAPER No 4 — Chester Archaeology

WEST CHESHIRE FROM THE AIR

AN ARCHAEOLOGICAL ANTHOLOGY

Best Wishes
Rhys Williams

S Rhys Williams

Chester
City Council

Published by Chester City Council
Department of Development and Leisure Services

ISBN 1 872587 11 9

Chester Archaeology
27 Grosvenor Street
Chester CH1 2DD
Tel: (01244) 402009
Fax: (01244) 347522
E-mail: j.hebblewhite@chestercc gov.uk
WWW: http://www.chestercc.gov.uk/
chestercc/htmls/heritage.htm

Printed by Bemrose Shafron Ltd,
11 Chaser Court, Greyhound Park,
Chester CH1 4QQ

THIS book does not pretend to be an exhaustive textbook on the history and archaeology of the west Cheshire landscape. Rather, it brings to the reader a selection of the observations and discoveries made by the author in twenty-five years of flying over the county.

Flying gives one an entirely new perspective on the countryside below. Instead of seeing individual places such as a village and a few fields, or perhaps a castle near a wood, the flyer sees the landscape as a whole. Individual sites are seen in the context of that landscape and relate to each other in a more intelligible way.

Apart from appreciating the whole picture, there is another advantage in observing a landscape from the air. In certain conditions, such as with a very low sun, or after a light fall of snow, or with corn which is just ripening, features, and even whole sites such as a deserted hamlet, can be revealed when they are not visible at all at ground level.

This book focuses upon west Cheshire, but not exclusively so. It has seemed right to include one or two other sites from other parts of Cheshire and just over the border in Wales and Shropshire when they illustrate particularly well developments also found in the west Cheshire landscape.

Some well known places, such as Beeston Castle, are in the care of English Heritage and are open to the public at advertised times. Others constitute private estates which may be open to the public on advertised dates. However, the majority of the sites illustrated are on private land and are not accessible without the express permission of the owner or the tenant farmer. Some sites have been noted in the text as Scheduled Ancient Monuments. This means they are protected under the Ancient Monuments and Archaeological Areas Act 1979. They are generally not accessible to the public because they are on private land. Those that are legally accessible will be clearly signposted with a footpath leading to the monuments. It must be stressed that it is illegal to use metal detectors at any Scheduled site or monument, or to interfere with them in any way without the written consent of the Secretary of State for National Heritage.

The aerial archaeologist uses several techniques for recognising ancient features in the landscape. Among them are noting continuous hedgerows which can often mark ancient routes (eg, Ills 23 and 24); noting transitory marks which can appear in crops, notably barley, in certain dry conditions (eg, Ill 28); and by observing shadows cast by a low sun, which will emphasize any slight hollow or bump which might otherwise not be visible (eg, Ill 64). Unlike in some other counties, cropmarks have not been numerous in Cheshire until recent years, as large areas have been kept under pasture for its renowned dairy herds. In recent years, however, there has been more ploughing and, predictably, cropmarks are more in evidence than they were, for example, ten years ago.

The camera used throughout was a Yashica TL-Electro with a 50 mm lens, a sky filter and a rubber lens hood. The film was usually an Ektachrome (now called Elite) ASA 200 or 400 (a colour slide film was preferred in order to illustrate talks and lectures). Most importantly, the aircraft was always a high-wing, single-engined, two- or four-seater Cessna. The high wing allows clear unimpeded vision of the ground; it also helps to shade the camera if photographs are taken into the sun. Most of the photographs were taken at heights between 700 and 1,500 feet.

The author hopes you will enjoy looking at his photographs and reading his notes as much as he has enjoyed selecting them and presenting them to you.

PREFACE

Contents

Acknowledgements

My first thanks must go to Mike Morris and Peter Carrington of Chester Archaeology for inviting me to write this book. I am also grateful to them for helping me to select the photographs and to Peter Carrington for his general guidance and management of the project. With them I would couple the names of Adrian Tindall and Jill Collens of Cheshire County Council for their advice and for giving me full access to the Sites and Monuments Record; also Dan Robinson of the Grosvenor Museum for his many valuable comments and suggestions on the text, likewise Ian Dunn for his valuable comments. I am grateful to Jane Hebblewhite for typing the first draft, Tim Morgan for producing the excellent drawings which help to interpret the photographs, Cheryl Quinn for the location maps and Alison Jones for help with copy-editing. My special thanks go to Captain Dave Williams and Deltair Limited; also to Messrs Tim Astbury, Roy Clark and Tom Henderson for their invaluable assistance.

I am grateful to the Rt Hon The Lord Mostyn and the University of Wales Bangor for permission to reproduce part of the Mostyn Estate map of Alpraham; to Cheshire County Council's Archives and Local Studies Service for permission to publish part of the tithe award map for South Bunbury; and to Adrian Tindall for permission to reproduce the photographs of the Churton mortuary enclosure and the Roman practice camp on Upton Heath.

Finally, but far from least, I would express my gratitude to those whose grant aid made this publication possible.

THE greater part of Cheshire is an extension of the midland plain which is seen in the neighbouring county of Staffordshire. The Cheshire part of this great plain extends from the foothills of the Pennines in the east to the steeply rising ground just beyond the River Dee in the west.

The Cheshire plain is divided by a central ridge of sandstone which rises dramatically at Larkton Hill near Broxton and continues with little peaks and dips, and a gap near Gallantry Bank, to Peckforton. Here it descends abruptly to the plain, only to reappear momentarily as the great defended rock of Beeston. At this point, there is a gap of about 4 km (about 2½ miles) until the ground begins to rise again near Tarporley. This high ground, which is too wide to be called a ridge, runs towards the north-west, meeting the River Mersey at Helsby and Frodsham. It then turns north-eastwards, ultimately to join the general uplands of the Pennine foothills in the area of Mottram and Macclesfield. The peninsula of Wirral, between the estuaries of the Dee and the Mersey, is also upland in character, with many areas of high ground, especially along its western side, and numerous outcrops of rock.

The rocks underlying the Cheshire plain mostly consist of Permian and Triassic sandstones with millstone grit along its eastern boundary, notably at Mow Cop. The two rock basins divided by the Central Ridge have been filled to considerable depths with various clays and glacial sands and gravels deposited during and immediately after the last Ice Age. The glaciers also deposited mounds of debris which give Cheshire a hummocky appearance, especially noticeable in the south near the border with Shropshire. Many of the meres found in this part of the county are the remnants of more extensive lakes and river systems which formed from the meltwaters of the receding glaciers.

Cheshire has four main river systems, all flowing in a north-westerly direction. Three of them, the Gowy, Weaver and Bollin, flow into the Mersey, but the Dee has its own estuary. Because of the wide range and level nature of the Cheshire plain the rivers tend to meander. This is especially the case with the Dee, which has a series of dramatic curves and loops in the vicinity of Farndon and Holt (Ill 6). The Dee has also formed 'ox-bow' lakes, which occur when a river winds so much that at last it cuts through the narrow neck of land between the bends, leaving crescent-shaped lakes or ox-bows. This has led to a curious political situation in the area between Shocklach Green and Caldecott Green. The boundary between England and Wales here has long followed the river, but has become fossilised on its old course. Consequently, although all the rest of the land to the west of the Dee is in Wales, three fields enclosed by the old meanders are in England.

1

THE NATURAL LANDSCAPE

Cholmondeston (Aston-juxta-Mondrum)

A landscape of several periods   NGR SJ 635577

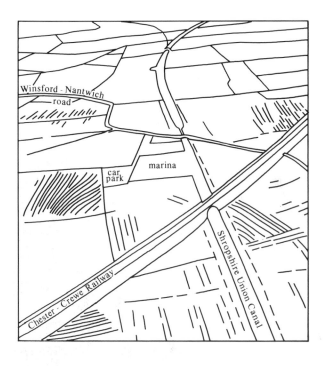

Ills 1-2 Cholmondeston
looking SW

The countryside resembles what students of ancient manuscripts call a palimpsest: that is, a parchment where one piece of writing has been imperfectly erased to make room for another, with the result that the original writing can still be made out.

So with the countryside, the activities of one period change or add to the landscape without ever fully obliterating what was there before. Photograph 2 is a simple example of this principle. It shows a stretch of countryside to the north of Nantwich. The photograph was taken in June 1977 and looks southwest. In reverse order of construction are a narrow-boat marina and car park in the centre of the photograph, which clearly belong to this century. Just below them, crossing the picture diagonally, runs the nineteenth-century railway line from Chester to Crewe. This in turn crosses the eighteenth-century Shropshire Union canal. The fields through which these features pass are irregularly shaped, suggesting that, for the most part, they are of seventeenth- or eighteenth-century date. Beneath the fields, and passing under many of the hedgerows but not clearly visible in the photograph, there is a curving ridge and furrow indicative of the ploughing of medieval open fields. Also, bridged over the canal, there is an unclassified road which links Winsford and Nantwich. Its winding nature and the right-angled bend just to the left of the marina strongly suggest that it, too, is of medieval date.

2

Peckforton

The Peckforton Hills (The Central Ridge)   **NGR SJ 535515** (centre of photograph)

This photograph, taken in July 1978, looks north towards the Central Ridge. Cholmondeley Castle, with its park and meres, is in the foreground. Behind is the village of Bulkeley, with Peckforton Castle and the detached rock of Beeston on the right.

In earlier times, when the Cheshire plain was more heavily wooded than it is now, part at least of the ridge is said to have been used by Welsh traders on their way to and from the salt town of Nantwich. It is unlikely that cattle herders would have used such a route except, perhaps, for a short distance. The climb to the top is quite steep and the ridgeway very uneven. Anyone driving a herd is likely to have chosen a less hazardous way. The route that suggests itself is the much more direct one that runs through the gap at Gallantry Bank, between Bickerton Hill and the slopes of Rawhead. This route leads directly to Broxton and thence to the crossing over the Dee at Farndon. Nevertheless, the names *Walesmonsway* (Welshman's way) and *Walchmanstreete* (Welshman's street) are said to have been applied to the ridgeway above Peckforton in the Middle Ages.

Subsidiary ridges and outliers run westwards from the main ridge near Bickerton, passing through Edge (a miniature of Alderley Edge) and Carden. The latter place has a prehistoric rock shelter or shallow cave. Its natural sandstone walls have in part been 'improved' by being smoothed and straightened, probably in the eighteenth or early nineteenth century judging by their appearance. There are also traces of an attempt to level the rough rock floor with a layer of cement. The slope running down from the shelter is riddled with rabbit burrows, and one or two small flakes of flint, which are foreign to the locality, were found at the entrance to one of them a short time ago. They were recognisable as waste from making flint tools and are believed to date to the Meso-

III 3 The Peckforton Hills, looking N

3

lithic period, or Middle Stone Age, which accompanied the improving climate and the spread of woodland after the last great glaciation. The shelter would have been convenient for a brief stop, perhaps overnight, and an excellent vantage point for any hunter watching game wandering about in the valley below (now Carden Park) and perhaps drinking unsuspectingly at the Carden Brook.

That the Central Ridge itself was traversed in antiquity cannot be doubted. There is an Iron Age hillfort, known as Maiden Castle, on Bickerton Hill. It commands extensive views along the ridge and especially towards the west, over the Dee, to the Clwydian hills. Rawhead is said to have been a site of a prehistoric settlement, although no amount of observation from the air has revealed it. One may, on occasion, observe periglacial features appearing as cropmarks, and these may have been incorrectly interpreted. However, the greater part of a curious rectangular ditched feature has been observed as a transitory cropmark. The most likely interpretation, especially given the nearness of the hillfort at Maiden Castle, is a small Celtic rectangular shrine, such as have been found elsewhere in Britain and on the Continent.

There is no direct evidence for an early occupation of Horsely Hill, upon which the nineteenth-century Peckforton Castle now stands, although there are some uncertain references to the Black Prince having repaired a castle in the vicinity, which was not necessarily at Beeston, and it is possible that this was a hunting lodge or a detached tower rather than a castle. Beeston Castle itself is built on the site of an Iron Age hillfort which incorporated an Early Bronze Age settlement.

The northern half of the Central Ridge, from Tarporley to Helsby, also has its ancient sites. These include the prehistoric promontory camp of Kelsborrow Castle at Kelsall; the great Iron Age hillfort, known as the Old Pale, at Eddisbury; Helsby Iron Age hillfort; and two smaller camps near Frodsham, one at Woodhouses and the other at Bradley.

The lands along the Central Ridge are the properties of many owners. Notable among them are the National Trust for Maiden Castle, and the Tollemache Estate for Peckforton and Beeston castles. The latter is now in the guardianship of English Heritage. By agreement between landowners and the various local authorities, *via* Cheshire County Council, much but by no means all of the ridge forms part of the well known Sandstone Trail. Those parts which are on the trail and accessible to the public are well signposted.

Dodcott-cum-Wilkesley

Comber Mere and Combermere Park   **NGR SJ 590445**

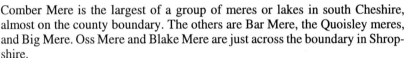

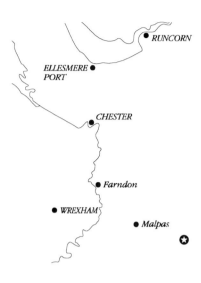

III 4 Combermere Park, looking NE

Comber Mere is the largest of a group of meres or lakes in south Cheshire, almost on the county boundary. The others are Bar Mere, the Quoisley meres, and Big Mere. Oss Mere and Blake Mere are just across the boundary in Shropshire.

These meres represent meltwater from the receding ice sheets of the last great glaciation which had been trapped by the debris forming the Ellesmere moraine, itself left behind by the ice. This morainic material effectively prevented the escape of water both to the Dee and to the Severn. Indeed, it was this same moraine that turned the Severn itself in a southerly direction.

Photograph 4, taken looking north-east, shows the crescent-shaped lake sitting serenely in the beauty of Combermere Park. The lake is not entirely natural, having been extended in the eighteenth century. Combermere Park is listed Grade II as being of architectural interest.

The area was probably difficult to traverse in antiquity and is rather isolated even now. Its name perhaps bears witness to this isolation, for Comber Mere means 'lake of the Cumbri' (or Welsh). This suggests that a pocket of Celtic-speaking Britons survived here for some time after the Anglo-Saxon conquest of the rest of the area, presumably eventually being absorbed into the developing kingdom of Mercia.

Later history is recorded in the name Combermere Abbey, the large house fronting onto the lake near the centre of the photograph. This house, whose architecture is reminiscent of Walpole's Strawberry Hill 'Gothic Revival' style, is deceptive. Much of what appears from a distance to be stonework carved in the Gothic style was discovered some years ago to be stucco which masked timber framing and wattle and daub construction. The house originally must have been a typical Cheshire black-and-white mansion. Even this was not the beginning of the story, for the house was presumably built on or near the site of the great Cistercian religious foundation of the same name. It was a rich and powerful abbey founded in 1133, with a number of churches under its control and several granges or monastic farms. It also had lucrative interests in the salt town of Nantwich. The exact position of the abbey was uncertain until the structure of the house was examined some twenty years ago. Immediately above the magnificent seventeenth-century moulded and painted plaster ceiling of the first-floor music room, finely moulded and carved roof trusses were found which were tentatively dated to the late fifteenth century. They were evidently meant to have been seen from the floor below. *(Continued on page 7)*

Church Shocklach

The River Dee **NGR SJ 417485** (centre of photograph)

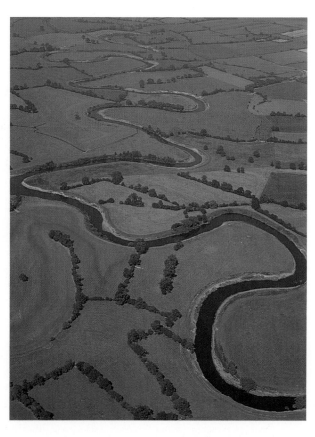

Ill 5 The River Dee at Church
Shocklach, looking N

Rising on the slopes of Dduallt, some 8 km (5 miles) beyond Bala Lake (Llyn
Tegid), the Dee is Cheshire's biggest river. Having flowed through the Vale of
Llangollen, it reaches the flat Cheshire plain not far from Erbistock. The Dee
begins to meander before it fully leaves the Vale of Llangollen and continues
to do so in large curving sweeps as far as Bangor-on-Dee (Bangor-is-y-Coed).
After Bangor its course becomes more contorted and tortuous, with the meanders forming tight loops for much of the way to Holt.

Photograph 5 was taken in July 1984, looking north towards Holt, 5.25 km
(2¾ miles) downstream.

The name 'Dee', which has essentially the same element as *Deva,* the
Roman name for Chester, is derived from a Celtic word meaning deity, probably a goddess. The word, in various guises, is common to most Indo-European
languages and is seen, for example in the Latin *dea* (a goddess) and the Welsh
'duw' (a god).

For many years the river downstream from Shocklach Green has been the
boundary between England and Wales. However, the Dee has formed many
ox-bows in the course of the years, and in some places the river has cut through
the neck of the bow, leaving the national boundary to follow the old meander.
We now therefore have the curious situation where the land to the west of the
Dee is in Wales except for three small fields (the old ox-bows) which are in
England.

The River Dee was at one time navigable for small craft from the estuary as
far upstream as Holt. This became impossible when the weir was built at Chester in the early Middle Ages. Small craft did, however, continue to ply between
Chester and Holt, apparently up to the seventeenth century if not later. A sunk-
en barge was recently found by divers near Holt and is said to be of a
seventeenth-century design.

Farndon and Holt

The River Dee   NGR SJ 400560 (centre of photograph)

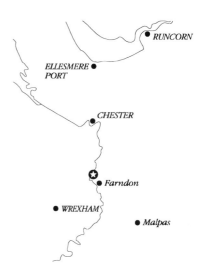

III 6 The River Dee at Farndon, looking SW

Photograph 6 was taken in August 1988 looking south-westwards. Just downstream from Farndon and Holt, the River Dee follows a quite remarkable course, doubling back on upon itself where it is joined by the River Alyn before turning again to follow its original course towards Chester and the sea. The River Alyn comes in from Rossett, but begins its long journey on a watershed on Llantysilio Mountain in the Clwydian range. After the spectacular loop seen in the photograph, the Dee becomes less meandering and has its final fling at the great Crook of Dee in Huntington. From there it goes on to the great curving sweeps around Chester's Meadows and the Roodee. Downstream from the Roodee, the river's course to the sea was changed by the 'New Cut', a straight channel made for it in the eighteenth century. While the Cut does not look particularly attractive, it was necessary as the old channel past Saughall and Shotwick had become unacceptably silted with sand, partly brought down by the Dee and partly resulting from erosion of the soft sandy cliffs fringing the estuary from Burton Point onwards.

Dodcott-cum-Wilkesley *(continued from page 5)*
It was concluded, on fairly sure grounds, that the roof was *in situ* and could have been that of a great hall, either of the refectory of the abbey or, more probably, of the abbot's lodgings.

The house known as Combermere Abbey (a Grade I Listed Building) is therefore without doubt the immediate successor to the Cistercian abbey which evidently stood on the same site. Upon the dissolution of the monasteries in 1538, King Henry VIII granted the property to Sir George Cotton. It is now believed that Sir George demolished the church and most of the old monastic buildings, but retained the abbot's great hall. Judging by its roof timbers, this hall had apparently been refurbished in the late fifteenth century, not long before Sir George acquired it.

The Dee Estuary

The 'New Cut' **(NGR SJ 396667)** and the reclamation of sea land   **(NGR SJ 250770)**

III 7 The Dee estuary from the Welsh shore, looking N to West Kirby and Hilbre Island

III 8 The beginning of the 'New Cut' at Chester, looking SW. Crane Wharf is off the picture to the left.

Chester was a port in Roman times, and the Dee estuary may have been a favoured landfall for Irish Sea traffic before that. In the Middle Ages, Chester was the main seaport north of Bristol for coastal trade, trade with Ireland and trade with Europe, especially in wine. However, there has always been a problem with the progressive silting up of the estuary, and this eventually led to a reduction of shipping using the port.

Chester was not the only port on the English side of the estuary, for both Burton and Shotwick were important during the Middle Ages. By the eighteenth century Parkgate had captured the Irish traffic and in the early 1800s it became a spa and popular sea-bathing resort. However, it too became badly affected by the silting of the estuary and gave way to Liverpool, which became the main port for the north-west.

The natural course of the River Dee downstream from Chester ran around the Roodee to Blacon, from where the main channel ran past Shotwick to Burton Point and beyond. The boundary between England and Wales still follows this line.

During the eighteenth century it became fashionable for entrepreneurs not only to enclose waste land and commons but also to reclaim sands and estuarine deposits as farming land. In order to do this, and hopefully revive Chester's fortunes as a port, a new straight channel (or cut) was made from near Crane Wharf to Connah's Quay. It then continued as a dredged channel through the estuary sands to Flint. This enabled several thousand acres of sand and poor quality estuary marsh to be reclaimed as usable land and is the origin of the name 'Sealand'.

The photograph of the estuary (Ill 7) was taken in 1980 between high and low tide. It shows West Kirby at the north-west tip of Wirral and Hilbre Island between it and the left-hand side of the picture.

Photograph 8, taken in February 1983, shows the dramatic change in direction of the River Dee where its old course meets the New Cut near Crane Wharf.

References
Carrington ed 1994, *passim*

Ellesmere Port (Stanlow)

Confluence of the Rivers Gowy and Mersey   NGR SJ 430775

Ill 9 The confluence of the Gowy and Mersey, looking SW

This rather dramatic photograph was taken looking south-west. The late afternoon sun reflecting off the water gives it a silvery appearance which contrasts with the dark colour of the silts and sands forming the Stanlow and Ince banks of the River Mersey. The banks are also in clear contrast to the Manchester Ship Canal, which may be seen as a long strip of clear water crossing the picture from left to right. As the photograph shows, it was cleverly engineered to pass over the River Gowy. The building of the ship canal was prompted by the gradual silting up of the Mersey and the Irwell, but its construction would in any case have been necessary in time if ships of any size, as opposed to barges, were to reach Manchester.

The River Gowy, once known as the Tarvin (Welsh 'terfyn' from Latin *terminus,* meaning a boundary), rises just south-east of Peckforton and flows due north to near Beeston. It then turns east, only to turn sharply north again at Bunbury. It then meanders in a north-westerly direction to reach the Mersey at Stanlow.

There are several places of archaeological interest along its route, apart from the rock of Beeston and its castle. There is an abandoned moated hall sited at Foulk Stapleford (Ill 60); the medieval pack-horse bridges, popularly known as the 'Roman Bridges', at Hockenhull; and Plemstall church, the probable site of the ninth-century St Plegmund's cell, is almost on its banks (Ill 33). ☞

Delamere

Post-glacial water channels on the slopes of Primrose Hill   **NGR SJ 543683**

III 10 Water channels on
Primrose Hill

About 12500 BC the ice of the last great glaciation of the northern hemisphere
finally retreated from Cheshire. The landscape it left behind was one of deposited boulders, clays and other morainic materials, over which tundra conditions
prevailed until woodland and then forest gradually spread to cover the area by
about 8000 BC.

As the snows and the ice of the glaciers retreated, a great deal of water was
left behind to form pools, rivulets and streams, all finding their way downhill to
form larger channels. These in turn fed the major rivers which were now taking
shape, such as the Dee, the Mersey and the Severn.

Some of the old post-glacial channels can still be seen during droughts, which
produce parch- or residual damp-marks in grass and cereal crops. Photograph
10, taken in July 1976, shows a good example of this. Two channels curve
towards the right of the picture and presumably merge together a little further
on (the confluence is no longer visible). The dark green colour is due to moisture being retained in the old channels. The light margins are probably caused
by the presence of sands and gravels deposited by formerly running water.

The old channels are generally following the contours at this point, but if
their whole length was visible, they would without doubt be seen to have edged
eastwards to link with what are now Darley Brook and Ash Brook which join
the River Weaver some 3 km (2 miles) south of Winsford.

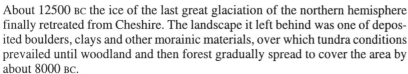

☞ At one time, the church was isolated on an island of dry land in the Gowy
marshes. The river has now been canalised, and a network of small channels
has helped to drain the marsh.

The Gowy meets the Mersey at the low-lying Stanlow Point (immediately to
the right of the Gowy in the photograph). A Cistercian abbey, built between
1172 and 1178, once stood here, but the site is now hidden by brushwood and
general undergrowth. It was always a desolate spot, typical, it seems, of all
Cistercian foundations, and one reached by a causeway across the marshes. It
can now only be reached by taking a ferry boat across the Manchester Ship
Canal. In 1279 floods cut off the abbey from the landward side for a considerable time. Not long after that the church tower collapsed, and in 1289 there was
a disastrous fire. It was this fire in particular that caused the monks to move to
Whalley Abbey, near Clitheroe in Lancashire, in 1296.

2

PREHISTORY

UNTIL recent years, the prehistory of Cheshire was little understood. Flints and other stone tools had been found at several places, and one or two hoards of bronze objects such as axes and spearheads had been discovered. A number of burial mounds believed to date to the Bronze Age (*c* 2500 BC-*c* 750 BC) could still be seen, and there was a handful of fortified sites, presumed to date from the Iron Age (*c* 750 BC-*c* AD 43), along the Central Ridge and the high ground between Delamere and the Mersey. The county was generally believed to have been very sparsely populated, even in the late prehistoric period leading up to the Roman occupation. This picture is now proving to be more apparent than real.

Recent finds of flint tools, for example on the shore of Tatton Mere, have confirmed that wandering hunters were active in the county around 4500 BC and doubtless earlier. Flints of broadly the same period are known from the northern parts of Wirral, while others have recently been found near a rock shelter or shallow cave in Carden Park.

Chance finds from the Neolithic period or New Stone Age (*c* 4500-*c* 2500 BC) are more numerous. This was the period when the practice of agriculture ushered in a more settled way of life. Dwelling sites of the period are not numerous in any county, but burials in megalithic tombs (ie, large chambered cairns) or under earthen long mounds are relatively common in western and southern counties. Until recently, the only site of this type known in Cheshire was the ruined tomb known as the Bridestones near Congleton. However, a short time ago aerial photography revealed what seems to be a mortuary enclosure (a site connected with funerary ritual) of the same period near Churton-by-Farndon. A third possible burial mound has also been located at Somerford near Congleton.

The stone-using agricultural period merged with the Early Bronze Age around 2500 BC. Round burial mounds or barrows dating to this period are relatively numerous in Cheshire. Many of these mounds were single isolated monuments, but others are now seen to be grouped together into small cemeteries, some of which, in turn, form part of a more extensive necropolis as, for example, in the area around Jodrell Bank. The burial mounds so far identified in west Cheshire form small groups of three or four. That at Seven Lows (ie, seven mounds) Farm in Delamere is unusually large for the area. A previously unknown group of three was recently identified at Carden.

The later Bronze Age (*c* 1500 - *c* 750 BC) saw less emphasis on elaborate ritual burial in mounds and an increase in flat unmarked cemeteries where the ashes of the cremated dead were interred in pottery urns. The period has all the appearance of having had a more secular society than existed previously. On the other hand, it saw a considerable increase in small hoards of fine metalwork being buried in the ground. This is a national phenomenon and by no means peculiar to Cheshire. It used to be thought that such hoards represented the stock-in-trade of itinerant bronzesmiths who buried scrap metal with a view to recovering it for melting down and reuse on their next visit to the area. This never seemed to be very practical, and it is now thought more likely that the objects, many of which were undamaged and not scrap metal, were buried as votive offerings to some spirit or deity. Many buried hoards have been found near water, and the practice may be related to the ritual throwing of objects into water as offerings during the Late Bronze Age and especially during the succeeding Iron Age. Probably the best known examples in Britain come from

Llyn y Cerrig Bach near Valley, Anglesey, and Flag Fen near Peterborough. It formed part of Celtic religious ritual during the Iron Age, and some authorities now consider that the first Celtic-speaking people arrived in Britain during the Bronze Age, before the use of iron was introduced, bringing the practice with them.

The Celts are more usually associated with the Iron Age. Their characteristics are well known through the descriptions of Greek and Roman writers and from archaeology. They were divided into a large number of tribes and were a rural people who occupied scattered homesteads rather than large villages or towns, although there were exceptions to this on the Continent and in some parts of Britain. The only sites which could be considered as large settlements in Cheshire were the hillforts and the defended camps of the period.

Hillforts belong to the Late Bronze and Early Iron ages (*c* 850 BC-AD 43). They are amongst the best known monuments of the period and are scattered throughout western Europe. Some had houses within them; some seem to have been corrals; others probably served a variety of purposes. All were defended by banks and ditches. A total of some 250 are strung along the English-Welsh border, occupying vantage points, guarding river crossings and the valleys giving access to the interior of Wales, or overlooking landfalls on the coast. Those in Cheshire seem to watch over a route along the Central Ridge and the high ground to the north of it. They are at Maiden Castle (Bickerton Hill), Beeston (underlying the later castle), Kelsborrow Castle (Kelsall), Castle Ditch (Eddisbury) and Helsby Hill. There were also smaller fortified camps on Woodhouses Hill and at Bradley (both near Frodsham) and at Oakmere (in Delamere), Peckforton Mere and Burton Point (Wirral).

Although, as mentioned above, many hillforts contained houses and other structures, it is not clear whether any of those in western Britain, including Cheshire, represented permanent dwelling sites or whether they were refuges in times of trouble. Some, perhaps, provided summer quarters for pastoralists taking advantage of upland pastures. In the greater part of upland Cheshire, however, the elevation of the land is not so great as to have warranted separate summer and winter dwellings of this sort.

It used to be though that Cheshire was very sparsely populated during the Iron Age, as in all the other prehistoric periods, but this is now less certain as aerial photography produces more evidence for the existence of the scattered homesteads typical of the period.

With the coming of the Romans, the names of the various native British tribes become known to us. The people who occupied what is now Cheshire were the Cornovii, whose main territory lay in Shropshire and what is now eastern Powys. Their neighbours to the north-east were the Brigantes, whose main lands were in Lancashire and Yorkshire. To the west, beyond the Dee, were the Deceangli, who exploited the rich mineral deposits, especially lead, of what was to become Flintshire.

Churton

Neolithic mortuary enclosure   **NGR SJ 411558**

Ill 11 Churton Neolithic mortuary
enclosure, looking NE

References
Longley 1987, 44, 46

A dark rectangular cropmark may be seen in the centre of the photograph just
below the corner of the wood. It measures about 33 x 18 m and has rounded
corners and a wide gap at its southern end. It has been identified as a probable
long mortuary enclosure of the Neolithic period (*c* 4500 BC - *c* 2500 BC).

It is believed that such enclosures were used for exposing the dead to the
elements before their bones were entombed under a large mound or barrow.
Sometimes the smaller enclosures were covered over by the mound and became part of the tomb, but some larger examples occur as uncovered monuments
in their own right.

The enclosure at Churton was first discovered by David Longley, then a
researcher with the Department of the Environment, in 1975. The present photograph (Ill 11) was taken by Dr Jill Collens of Cheshire County Council and
Dr Rob Philpott of the National Museums and Galleries on Merseyside. They
report that the feature may be surrounded by an even larger rectangular enclosure. Other faint cropmarks suggest that there may be a similar enclosure in an
adjoining field.

The discovery is of prime importance to the prehistory of the county and
throws considerable light on early funerary practices in Cheshire.

Oswestry

Old Oswestry Iron Age hillfort   **NGR SJ 295310**

III 12 Old Oswestry Iron Age
hillfort, looking E

Oswestry is in Shropshire, but this hillfort is well worth including as it is very accessible and shows all the characteristics of such sites.

Photograph 12, taken in January 1979 looking east, shows that, as was often the case, Old Oswestry hillfort was not built on the summit of a high hill but occupies a drumlin or mound of glacial debris on otherwise relatively flat ground. Excavation showed that it contained numerous round houses, which were dated to the Bronze Age. This does not necessarily place the hillfort itself in that period. In all probability, it is an example of an earlier site being fortified during the Iron Age. Indeed, some of the houses may in reality have belonged to the early Iron Age, for round houses, as opposed to sub-circular structures, are largely a phenomenon of that age.

As can be seen in the photograph, the site was well defended, having no less than seven high earth banks and four or five ditches on the vulnerable north (left) side. The main entrance, on the west side, was also well defended. It appears in the photograph as a narrow defile rising uphill, passing between the earth banks which would have been stockaded. At the top, where it reached the innermost bank, there would have been a strong wooden gate giving access to the hillfort's interior. Part of a rather similar but shorter access way can be seen at the opposite side of the fort, but it is a little doubtful if this was an original entrance.

As may be seen, the defensive banks at the front of the hillfort are spread out, leaving room for several short cross banks. It has been suggested that the enclosed depressions thus formed were intended for collecting rain water. This may have been so given the absence of a well or spring of water within the hillfort itself

Status
Scheduled Ancient Monument

References
Forde-Johnston 1976, 172

Delamere

Eddisbury Iron Age hillfort and Saxon *burh*   **NGR SJ 553694**

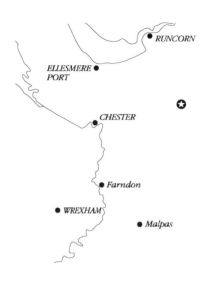

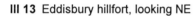

III 13 Eddisbury hillfort, looking NE

Cheshire's largest hillfort is also known as Castle Ditch or the Old Pale (ie, enclosure). It is sited in a prominent position on the eastern slopes of the Central Ridge and commands sweeping views to the north, east and south.

Photograph 13, taken in August 1981 looking north-eastwards to Delamere Forest, shows its main features. The outline of the fort is clear as an oval extending from Old Pale Farm on the left (west) side to the small wood on the right (east) side. It is defined by the curving hedge on the left and by its exposed bank and ditch at the bottom right (south-east) sector near the wood. The northern side, which is beyond the brow of the hill, has double banks and ditches. The second curving hedge, near the centre of the fort, almost certainly follows the line of an additional rampart. This possibly defined the western side of a smaller, earlier phase in the fort's history. Alternatively, it may have had two enclosed areas as, for example, did the hillforts on Conwy Mountain (Gwynedd) and at Pontesbury (Salop). These are known as multiple enclosure sites and are not uncommon.

Yet another rampart can be seen faintly some distance within the western end of the fort, between the two curving hedges. This inner rampart has an inturned entrance at its western end, opposite a gap in the outer rampart. Excavations carried out during 1935-8 showed that this inturned entrance and gateway had been revetted with timber. There had also been a strong gate pivoted on sturdy posts, whose charred stumps remained in their sockets. There were also guard chambers and other important constructions. There seems to have been a secondary entrance at the eastern end of the hillfort, where there is now a small wood, and yet another on the south-eastern side where the earth and stone ramparts are exposed and unhedged.

Photographs taken from the north suggest that a number of cultivation terraces or lynchets were associated with the hillfort, so it seems to have been occupied as a settlement rather than just a place of refuge. Lynchets may also have existed on the southern side, but activity in the Roman and medieval periods could have destroyed them (a major Roman road passes immediately to the south).

The Eddisbury hillfort was refortified in the tenth century AD, hence its name '-bury' or *-burh*, signifying a fortified enclosure. This was done by the Saxon queen Aethelflaed, daughter of King Alfred, and her brother Edward the Elder in 914 as part of their programme to secure the region from Danish and Norse raids. Chester itself had been refortified in 907, with *(continued on page 18)*

Status
Scheduled Ancient Monument

References
Longley 1987, 110-11
Varley 1950
Varley *et al* 1940, 65

Beeston

Iron Age hillfort and medieval castle   **NGR SJ 538592**

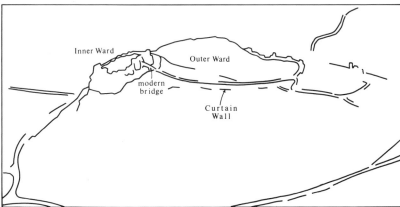

Ills 14-15 Beeston Castle, looking N

Beeston Castle is a prominent landmark, visible from many miles away, as any pilot of a light aircraft will testify. Photograph 16, taken under snow conditions in January 1979, shows this very clearly.

The castle, occupying the summit of a great detached rock, commands a gap in the Central Ridge. It was built in the thirteenth century by Ranulf III, Earl of Chester (1181-1232). Having been an important, indeed a major, castle in its heyday, it later played an important part in the Civil War.

Photograph 14, taken in December 1982 from a height of 700-800 feet, shows the sloping area occupied by the castle. The keep takes the form of a small, heavily fortified inner ward perched on the highest point of the rock and on the edge of a very steep slope. This inner ward is separated from the remainder of the very large walled area (or outer ward) by a wide and deep rock-cut ditch. The modern curving reinforced concrete bridge may be seen in the photograph leaping over the chasm.

It has only been discovered within the last few years that the hill at Beeston was also occupied, and fortified, in the prehistoric period. It is now clear that it should be counted amongst Cheshire's Iron Age hillforts, as well as being the site of a Bronze Age settlement. A series of archaeological excavations during the 1980s not only produced new facts about the medieval castle but also revealed defensive banks, fragments of roadways, cobbled areas and the postholes of wooden structures of the Iron Age. In addition, bronze-working was in evi-

Status
Scheduled Ancient Monument in the guardianship of English Heritage

References
Ellis 1993, *passim*
Hough 1982
Longley 1987, 105-7

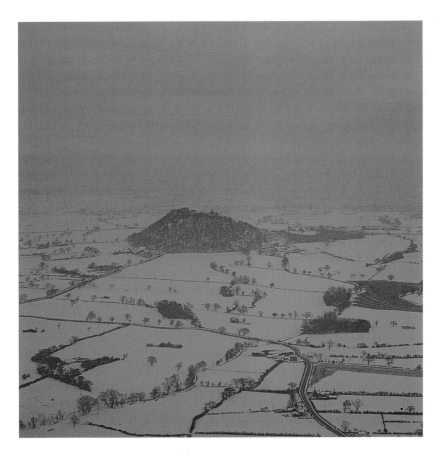

Ill 16 Beeston Castle in the snow, looking NE

dence as was pottery and other objects of the later phase of the Bronze Age. Illustration 14 shows the site of some of these excavations within the large outer ward appearing as a light-coloured rectangle between the wood at the summit of the hill and the curving path leading up to the bridge at the keep.

Delamere (*continued from page 16*)
the walled area being strengthened and perhaps enlarged. The site at Eddisbury was examined before World War II, and it is a little difficult to decide, without the benefit of modern excavation and dating techniques, what belongs to which period. It is comparatively easy to identify distinctive Iron Age features such as inturned entrances with timber revetting, round or half-round guard houses and timber tower structures. Even so, there are uncertainties remaining as to the precise extent of the tenth-century work, but it seems that at the least the ditches were recut and ramparts strengthened

There has been considerable disturbance of the hillfort since the tenth century, with structures being built against and upon the ramparts in the Middle Ages, with the Old Pale Farm complex being added in modern times. Quarrying has also taken its toll, both of the ramparts and the interior. For example, the small clump of trees seen within the fort is growing on one side of a sizeable former quarry.

Kelsall

Kelsborrow Castle promontory fort   **NGR SJ 532676**

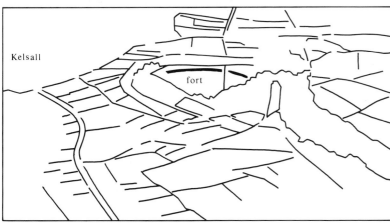

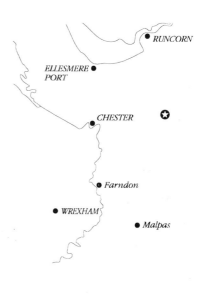

Ills 17-18 Kelsborrow Castle, looking N

While Eddisbury Hill and Beeston may be properly called hillforts, Kelsborrow Castle, Oakmere and Burton Point may fairly be classed as promontory forts or camps, occupying tongues of land jutting out into water or into the Cheshire plain. In the case of Kelsborrow Castle, it is a small promontory jutting out from the Central Ridge above Kelsall.

Photograph 17 was taken in August 1983 looking north towards the centre of Kelsall, with Delamere Forest in the distance. The promontory is in the very centre of the photograph. It commands views over the Cheshire plain to the west and along the slopes of the ridge to the Beeston Gap in the south. The slope of the ground would have afforded protection on the south and west sides, but to the north the land is at the same height as the fort. To protect the fort from attack, the promontory was effectively isolated on this side by a curving bank and ditch. There were originally two gaps in these ramparts giving access to the interior.

A small-scale archaeological excavation was carried out here some twenty years ago by an amateur team working under professional guidance, but unhappily the detailed results have never been published.

It is not known whether or not this fort was permanently occupied. A small prehistoric field system ('Celtic fields') is said to be associated with it, but the author has never been able to identify it from the air.

Status
Scheduled Ancient Monument

References
Longley 1987, 108, 111-13

Delamere

Oakmere promontory fort   **NGR SJ 576678**

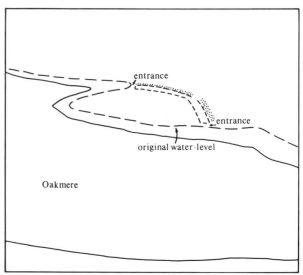

Ills 19-20 Oakmere promontory
fort, looking N

References
Longley 1987, 103, 116

Oak Mere is one of a string of small post-glacial lakes or meres in the Delamere
Forest area. A sand and gravel spit juts out into the lake from its eastern shore.

Photograph 19, taken in September 1979 looking north over the mere, shows
the promontory which was fortified in the prehistoric period, almost certainly
in the Early Iron Age. The defences consist of a bank and ditch which describe
an arc across the neck of the promontory, making access from the landward
side difficult for an attacker. These features are visible in the photograph,
albeit rather disguised by the bushes growing near them.

The defensive bank and ditch do not meet the present shoreline at their northern or southern ends, probably because the water level has dropped away from
them during the millennia. The original water level probably coincided with
the top of the slope now running down to the water's edge. The northern ends
of the bank and ditch come up to the top of this slope. At the southern end,
however, there is a narrow gap between them; this is believed to have been the
original entrance into the fort. There is a gap halfway along the bank which
coincides with a causeway over the ditch, but these are not thought to be
ancient.

Burton (Wirral)

Burton Point promontory fort   **NGR SJ 302736**

III 21 Burton Point promontory fort, looking NE

Unlike the promontory forts at Kelsborrow Castle and Oakmere, this one protrudes into the sea or, more accurately, into the estuary of the River Dee. Photograph 21, taken in February 1983, looks across the Wirral to the River Mersey in the distance. The wooded village of Burton is to the centre left of the photograph, and the promontory fort is at the bottom centre on the shoreline.

The fort occupies a slight rocky promontory which looks south and west over what was the main channel of the Dee before the New Cut was made in the eighteenth century. There is a very marshy area of partly reclaimed land beneath the fort, but when the fort was built the waters of the Dee would have come right up to rocky cliffs below it.

The site never seems to have been sampled archaeologically but is presumed from its character to be of Early Iron Age date. It was isolated on the landward side by a bank and ditch, which, as at Oakmere and Kelsborrow Castle, describe an arc across the neck of the promontory. The area now enclosed is very small indeed, but this probably belies its original extent. There has undoubtedly been much erosion on this coast, and quarrying has affected the site. It is said that some of the sandstone used in the building of Flint Castle, across the estuary, came from here.

There is no evidence as yet to suggest who or what the camp was protecting or guarding. If nothing else, it could have kept a watchful eye on traffic on the Dee and given warning if any unwelcome craft passed on their way upstream.

Status
Scheduled Ancient Monument

References
Longley 1987, 106, 109-10

21

3

THE ROMAN
PERIOD

THERE is no record of the Roman armies having to fight their way into the Cheshire area, nor of the local tribesmen having put up any resistance. Unlike some other British tribes, they seem to have accepted the presence of the invaders and carried on with their own way of life, largely maintaining their traditions, their Celtic religion and doubtless much else that distinguished them from the Romans. No doubt the invaders also accepted the situation as long as there was no political unrest or opposition to Roman requirements.

This situation could not last indefinitely. Cheshire formed a buffer between the potentially troublesome Ordovices of west and central Wales and the actively rebellious Brigantes to the east and north. In addition, Cheshire formed a useful corridor between the more settled Roman world and two important frontier areas where minerals could be exploited. These were the lead- and silver-producing area of north-east Wales and the copper-producing area of northern Anglesey, where copper is known to have been mined as early as the Middle Bronze age (c 1500 BC).

North-west Cheshire also has good access to the sea, suggesting the possibility of maritime control and trade. It is not surprising, therefore, that the legionary fortress of *Deva* (Chester) was founded there about AD 79. The fortress was sited on a bend of the River Dee at its highest navigable point, where there was also an easy river crossing for road traffic. The civil potential was considerable, but its initial importance would have been military. Chester was the centre of a network of forts controlling North Wales and the western Pennines. Many of these could be reached not only by the roads that the Romans built but also by ships sailing along the coast and up the many deeply penetrating estuaries that characterise the area. A fleet sailing from *Deva* could support any land troops moving northwards along the western side of Britain.

With the development of forts and a road network, the character of the area changed considerably. Industry and trade on a large scale were introduced. Wilderspool near Warrington seems to have been the largest Roman industrial settlement in what is now Cheshire. Not only was pottery made there, but there is a great deal of evidence for iron- and bronze-working. Pottery was also made at Northwich, Middlewich and Chester. The great tile and pottery works at Holt, across the river from Farndon, are well known. Salt was extracted from brine at Middlewich *(Salinae)*, Northwich *(Condate)* and to a lesser extent at Nantwich, whose Roman name is unknown. Copper had been mined at Alderley Edge as early as the Bronze Age; it was probably also mined by the Romans, but there is no proof of this.

Cheshire has only produced one building so far that could be classed as a villa, at Eaton-by-Tarporley. There are, as yet, no other proven Roman houses in the Cheshire countryside, but finds of fragments of dressed stone, brick, plaster and similar building materials of Roman character, (for example, at St Alban's Church, Tattenhall) suggest sites for other villas.

Chester

Upton Heath military practice camp **NGR SJ 418695**

III 22 Upton Heath practice camp, looking NE

This photograph, taken in August 1990 by Dr Jill Collens of Cheshire County Council and Dr Rob Philpott of the National Museums and Galleries on Merseyside, shows the cropmark of a large ditched enclosure with rounded corners and shaped like a playing card. The north-west corner lies under the water tower, and a marl pit has interrupted one long side. The mark occurred in a crop of barley, which is particularly good for producing cropmarks of this kind.

The enclosure, which was first seen by Dr Nick Higham of Manchester University, is one of several that have recently been discovered on the outskirts of Upton and Hoole. All the available evidence of size, shape and the profile of the ditch point to these being typical Roman practice camps.

It was essential that Roman soldiers acquired and maintained skills in building fortified camps at short notice with the available materials. Usually this meant laying out and constructing a sizeable camp surrounded by turf banks and a deep ditch with protected entrances. Apart from speed of construction, there was a special skill required in building rounded corners and protected entrances out of turf.

Many of these practice camps, as they are known, have been recognised throughout Wales and in northern Britain, some near Hadrian's Wall, and there is a group just outside York. Sometimes, something more elaborate than practice camps was attempted; practice forts, as opposed to camps, have been recognised at Cawthorn in Yorkshire. No doubt the sites at Upton and Hoole were the work of soldiers based in the fortress at Chester.

References
Cheshire Sites & Monuments Record
Frere 1987, 214-15
Frere & St Joseph 1983, 136-7

Churton-by-Farndon

Road line   **NGR SJ 428572** (centre of photograph)

III 23 Road line at
Churton-by-Farndon, looking SE

References
Petch 1987, 216-18
Waddelove & Waddelove 1983
Williams 1978/9, pl 3, for another
portion of this hedge line

This photograph, taken looking south-east in September 1977, shows a long straight hedge planted sometime in the past along the Roman road running between Chester and Whitchurch (*Mediolanum*).

It is a fine example of how the position of antiquities can be preserved in the landscape for centuries by such things as hedgerows. It also emphasizes the importance of retaining unusual hedges such as this, at least until it has been ascertained what it is that they mark.

This is the Roman road which left Chester and crossed over the river near to where the Old Dee Bridge now stands. It ran through Eaton Park, crossing the Dee again at Aldford, where it skirted the site of the later castle. The road has been traced passing through Stretton, the 'settlement on the street' (ie, a Roman road). After Stretton, it changed direction to head for Malpas and then Whitchurch and the south. Fieldwork shows that there are, in fact, two Roman roads which ran side by side for at least 8 km, one presumably superseding the other. Remarkably, the long hedge marks the position of the slighter of the two roads.

Contrary to popular belief, Roman roads do not maintain their proverbial straightness for the whole of their lengths. There are several slight changes of direction in this road, and one of them can be seen just above the centre of the photograph. The hedge coming into the picture at the centre left follows the course of the Plowley Brook. Where the two hedges converge, the Roman ☞

Stamford Bridge

Road line   **NGR SJ 474674** (centre of photograph)

Photograph 24, looking north-east, shows the A51(T) road coming in from Chester at the bottom left-hand corner. The road is quite straight, and in that respect typically Roman, between Boughton and Stamford Bridge (the group of buildings at centre-left of the photograph). When it reaches Stamford Bridge, the A51(T) bends to the right around Holme Bank and then forks left near Tarvin, now as the A54(T), and heads for Kelsall, Delamere and beyond.

The Roman road, however, did not bend significantly and carried on from Stamford Bridge straight up Kelsall hill. This Roman road line is clearly marked in the photograph by the long straight hedge, which starts just beyond Stamford Bridge and heads for the top right-hand corner of the photograph. By chance, or by good design, the recently built by-pass up Kelsall hill follows the Roman route, and the hedge cannot now be seen. Evidently our present-day highway engineers agreed with their Roman predecessors that this was by far the best and most economical route.

This Roman road, represented by the A54(T) and the long hedge, was known in medieval times as Watling Street; scholars now know it as Margary Route 7a. It linked Chester (*Deva*) with the forts at Northwich (*Condate*) and Manchester (*Mamucium*). It also linked Chester, *via* Route 70a, with the large Roman industrial complex at Wilderspool near Warrington and the salt-working settlement at Middlewich (*Salinae*).

III 24 Road line at Stamford Bridge, looking NE

References
Margary 1957, 33-6
Petch 1987, 218-20

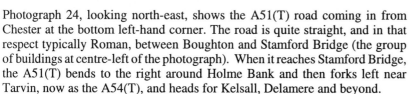

road bends to the right. According to measurements taken from the Ordnance Survey map published in 1954, the hedge marking the Roman road was unbroken for a distance of 3 km (about 1¾ miles). Generally speaking, it is still continuous, but one significant gap was created a few years ago.

The road was a substantial barrier to ploughing. It is therefore not surprising that a hedge was planted along it; also, the parish boundary between Coddington and King's Marsh follows it for a considerable distance.

Eaton-by-Tarporley

Villa **NGR SJ 572634**

Ill 25 Eaton villa, looking E

Photograph 25, taken in July 1982 looking east, illustrates well the difficulty of identifying small sites from the air, especially in an inhabited area. The minimum height at which an aircraft is permitted to fly over such an area is 1,200 feet. The photograph was taken from about 1,400 or 1,500 feet, which was a little too high in this case to see anything significant.

The villa site was being excavated when the photograph was taken. It can be made out as a rectangular patch in the small paddock immediately to the left of some long buildings at the very centre of the picture. It is the only Roman villa found in Cheshire so far, although there are hints of one or two others.

Structural remains of Roman character and a Roman coin were found at this spot in 1886 when the water main from Lake Vyrnwy to Liverpool was laid through the south-eastern corner of the villa. They did not seem to arouse a great deal of interest at the time, and the discovery was forgotten. However, its significance was ultimately realised by Dr D J P Mason, who was carrying out research at Liverpool University. He determined to investigate the area, and this resulted in the rediscovery of the building and its excavation between 1980 and 1982.

As was the case with many villas, this one began as a rectangular timber building, of which there were two phases. Both were almost impossible to date because of the shortage of datable finds. However, the little evidence available points to the site being occupied around AD 150

About 170 the timber buildings were replaced by a single-storey rectangular stone building, facing south-east with a wing at both ends and an open colonnade between them. The southern wing comprised a bath suite of three rooms and a furnace for under-floor heating (hypocausts). The northern wing also consisted of three rooms, two of which had hypocausts and a furnace. There were five rooms in the main building, one of which (probably the dining room) had a heated floor and an outside furnace. During this phase the villa, while not opulent, was extremely well constructed with solid stone walls and stone shingles and clay tiles on the roofs.

In the late third or early fourth century the villa was remodelled. Most of the building remained as it was in plan, but the open colonnade was replaced by a solid wall and the area apparently incorporated into the house. Also the central heating of the dining room and of two rooms in the north wing was discontinued, but the bath suite in the south wing continued to function as before. Several of the outer walls of the villa were thickened during this phase, presumably to carry an upper storey. It is also interesting to note that slate largely replaced tiles and stone shingles as the roofing material. Finds showed that the villa continued to be occupied well beyond AD 350.

The site was ideally suited for a villa. It faced south-east into the morning sun and must have commanded extensive views. The villa was sheltered from northerly and westerly winds by the hill behind it. A fine spring of clear water, which formed a little rivulet coming down the hillside, still exists. There would doubtless have been other buildings associated with the house. These have not been found but are presumed to lie under the adjoining modern properties. Long after the Roman occupation had been forgotten, the site was used for a complex of fourteenth-century kilns and their stoking pits, from which large quantities of pottery wasters were recovered.

References
Mason 1982, 1983
Petch 1987, 210-11

Claverton

Enclosure and site at Heronbridge   **NGR SJ 412637**

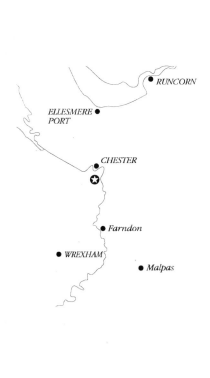

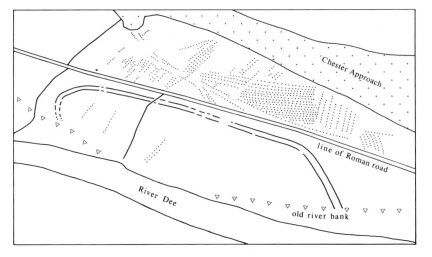

Ills 26-7 Enclosure and site at Heronbridge, looking SW

The photograph of the enclosure at Heronbridge was taken in June 1983 and looks south-west over the Dee and Eaton Road, which runs from Chester to Eccleston. The line of trees at the top of the photograph marks the drive to Eaton Hall known as the Chester Approach. This begins at the Overleigh roundabout in Handbridge and is now severed by the Chester southerly by-pass before it reaches Eccleston and Eaton Park.

The ancient enclosure is very elongated and stretches from the crescent-shaped line of trees on the left almost to the right-hand corner of the picture. The enclosure has aroused considerable speculation over many years as to its date and purpose, being variously identified as a Roman construction, the site of the Battle of Chester in AD 616 and more recently as a seventeenth-century Civil War defensive enclosure.

The Royal Commission on Historic Monuments in England has recently surveyed the feature on the ground and have concluded that it is not an enclosure as such, although the site was occupied in the Roman period. The Commission accept that there is a crescent-shaped bank at its southern end, but say that the long bank on the west is not continuous. The photograph does seem to show a break about halfway along its length. The Royal Commission also claim that

28

3: The Roman period

much of the bank is merely an unusually pronounced headland left by plough-ing. Whether these arguments are valid or not is open to discussion. The aerial photograph strongly suggests that the enclosure starts at the old river bank at its southern end, curves round, follows Eaton Road, and then moves in towards the river again to meet the old river bank at its northern end.

Human remains were found at this site during archaeological excavations in the 1930s, including several complete skeletons. All those examined proved to be male and many had injuries to their skulls, which suggested they had been cut down by horsemen, presumably cavalrymen. Their burial without ceremony pointed to the aftermath of a battle or at the very least a skirmish. The bones suggested to some that the site was that of the Battle of Chester but no date was ever ascribed to the burials. They could have belonged to any period from the late Roman to the Civil War.

Excavations have shown that the Roman road which left Chester by its south gate lay immediately to the east of Eaton Road. Its remains have been found between that road and the west bank of the ancient enclosure. The road passed through a Roman settlement which extended for about 300 m (1,000 feet) along its eastern side and for at least 60 m (200 feet) on its western side. A number of buildings have been located, if not fully excavated, and quantities of potsherds and other materials recovered. There may well be other buildings further removed from the Roman road.

References
Laing & Laing [1985], 8-19
Mason 1988
Petch 1975
Petch 1987, 188-92

Utkinton

Possible villa or farmstead

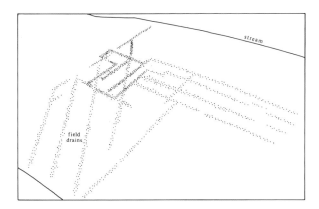

Ills 28-9 Possible Roman villa or farmstead at Utkinton

Photograph 29, taken in June 1983, is a fine example of an enigmatic cropmark whose interpretation could only be achieved by trial excavation or at the very least fieldwalking to recover datable objects.

The cropmarks in this field are of two, or probably three, periods. All the linear marks represent trenches or furrows rather than buried foundations. The diagonal lines are clearly modern field drains, while most of the dark green lines running parallel with the hedge probably represent post-medieval ridge and furrow ploughing. In both cases, the dark tone of the lines is caused by residual moisture in the furrows and drainage trenches. Similarly, the dark patches are caused by residual moisture in the soil keeping the growing crop green, while that elsewhere in the field is ripening.

There remain unexplained the dark rectangular cropmark lines towards the left of the photograph. They are crossed by the diagonal lines of the field drains and are unconnected with them. They could conceivably be the lines of earlier drains linking together a number of damp patches for discharge into a ditch. However, this usually produced a haphazard pattern, while the features in the photograph consist of one basic and several subsidiary rectangles. Solid walls beneath the surface could be expected to produce light-coloured marks in the crop. It is suggested, therefore, that the pattern represents either the foundation trenches of a building from which the stone has been robbed, or the lines of drainage channels that ran around a building. It could be a mixture of the two. The size of the pattern suggests a barn or something similar, but an isolated barn seems a little unlikely at this spot. There is no evidence for a recent (ie, post-World War I) building here.

It is tentatively suggested that the cropmarks represent part of a small Roman villa complex or farming establishment. The long axis of the cropmarks runs east-west, giving the building a north or south main aspect, surely the latter. This would have meant a building facing down the slight slope towards the south. There is running water in a nearby stream, which has no doubt existed for centuries, and there are probably springs in the area. The site would therefore have been quite acceptable for a group of agricultural buildings in the Roman period. In contrast, it could be argued that the necessity for field drainage in recent times probably precludes its use for a dwelling in times past. This does not necessarily follow: what applies today may well not have applied fifteen hundred or more years ago.

THE period popularly called the Dark Ages or the Invasion Period followed the year 410, when the Britons were instructed by Rome to fend for themselves. It was a period of great unrest, with emerging nations looking for living space and migrating into and across Europe. Rome, in consequence, was beset on all sides by enemies. In Britain, settlers were coming across the Irish Sea into Wales; Scandinavians were moving south along the coasts of Scotland, Ireland and Wales; and Germanic tribes from the Low Countries (the Anglo-Saxons) were moving into south-eastern Britain. Organised government from Rome had broken down and the Britons, including what remained of the Roman army in Britain, had to see to their own affairs. There was no longer any direction or support from beyond the Channel, no appeals to Caesar or any financial help for the foreseeable future. However, Rome had left one very important legacy, namely a developing Christian religion which had been introduced into Britain by Roman believers and their families. Christian emblems found at several Roman villas and other establishments in Britain illustrate this.

Britain in the Roman period was, in effect, divided into two zones. The first was the Romanised lowland area, comprising the midlands, the east and the south of the country. The second was the much less Romanised highland areas of the north and west. This division was reflected in the Dark Ages. The lowland areas fairly soon became Anglo-Saxon and pagan in character, although some pockets of Romano-British culture and language lingered on for a while. For example, the British kingdom of Elmet, around Leeds, and some of the people of the East Anglian fens spoke in a British Celtic dialect almost until the coming of the Normans.

The more traditional and persistently Celtic highland area stretched from Strathclyde in the north, through Cumbria to Wales and its border counties, on to Devon and Cornwall in the south. In these areas dialects of the British tongue persisted, as did the Christian religion. Curiously, these Celtic speakers of the west did not so much regard themselves as Celtic but as the sole survivors of the great Roman world. They saw themselves as the defenders both of the rapidly vanishing culture of the Romans and of the Christian faith.

The Romans had never conquered Ireland. Nevertheless, Christianity arrived there quite early, probably through the efforts of Welsh missionaries, and the Irish soon became the main influence on the development of insular Christianity. Ireland had a very great number of monasteries (perhaps the successors to pagan druidic colleges), which were in close contact with monasteries in Italy and through them with the Coptic Church in Egypt. The Irish welded together elements of pagan Celtic, Scandinavian, Anglo-Saxon and Coptic art to produce the superb Anglo-Hibernian art of illuminated manuscripts such as the Book of Kells, the Lindisfarne and Lichfield Gospels and others.

The flourishing Christianity of Ireland flooded back to Britain in the days of such great personalities as St Patrick, St David, St Columba, St Chad and many others. There are echoes of this in the Sandbach crosses, which are believed to be derived from Northumbrian Christian art, which was in turn directly inspired by Irish missionary effort.

Many Christian churches, including several in Cheshire, are dedicated to St Chad. Such a dedication, and a round or curvilinear churchyard, are sure signs of a church founded during the Dark Ages. There are other signs of early Christian churches to be found in place-names. For example, Christleton and

THE DARK AGES

Eccleston (the settlement where there was an *ecclesia,* ie, a church).

The main body of Celtic-speaking sub-Roman Britons (eventually to become the Welsh) was plainly to the west of the River Dee, with lowland Cheshire being drawn into the Anglo-Saxon world fairly quickly, ultimately to become part of the English kingdom of Mercia. Nevertheless, some place-names suggest that pockets of Celtic-speaking families remained for some time before being absorbed into the greater English-speaking community. Examples are Combermere and Comberbach, where 'Comber-' means 'Welshmen'.

The English-speaking people of Mercia had different traditions from the earlier Celtic- (Welsh-) speaking inhabitants. They seem to have introduced open-field agriculture with land holdings in the form of long arable strips, predominantly for corn growing, the whole system being based upon nucleated villages or hamlets. The older British (Celtic) tradition was one of mixed farming with fairly small enclosed fields and scattered homesteads. It has often been said that the open lands of Cheshire and some other western counties were enclosed into fields at an early date. This may well be the result of tradition and habit persisting from an earlier age.

Bangor-on-Dee

Site of monastery   **NGR SJ 389455**

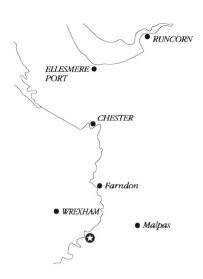

III 30 Bangor-is-y-Coed, looking E

Bangor-on-Dee, or Bangor-is-y-Coed in Welsh, is now in Wrexham County Borough. Before 1974 it was in the detached portion of Flintshire. It played an important part in the early relationship between Chester and the Welsh kingdom of Powys. This kingdom seems to have been based on the territory of the ancient British tribe of the Cornovii, which included what was later to become Cheshire.

The Welsh name Bangor-is-y-Coed is a topographical one and means the Bangor which was 'below (or lower down than) the trees'. The name Bangor is also interesting. It is a common enough word in Welsh and means a wattled fence or a hurdle. Early British monastic foundations were enclosed within such fences and so, by association, 'bangor' also came to mean a monastery. There was an important Dark Age monastery at Bangor-on-Dee. Along with its namesake in Gwynedd, it was founded by St Deiniol in the sixth century. Both were patronised and endowed with lands by the kings of both Gwynedd and Powys, and the leading members of their monastic communities played important parts in the politics of the two kingdoms.

In the seventh century the kingdom of Northumbria began to expand aggressively and its armies reached the west midlands. The Mercians and the eastern Welsh joined forces to oppose the northern armies. The Welsh of Powys were the nearest defenders available and they met the Northumbrians in 616 or 617. The Welsh forces needed all the help they could get, and that quickly, against the might of Northumbria, and the help of the monks of Bangor-on-Dee was enlisted. This situation should cause no surprise, as many of the monks were probably lusty soldiers who had retired, if only temporarily, into a monastery. In the event, the battle was lost with many casualties to the men of Powys, over a thousand of the monks of Bangor-on-Dee being slain.

No features from that time are visible today. The aerial photograph is one of several taken in August 1988. It shows the medieval bridge spanning the Dee (bottom centre) and the new road bridge at the right of the picture. The church is on the riverside, immediately to the right (south) of the old bridge.

The village, which shows nothing of its important past, is sited on one of the many bends of the river on low-lying land which has always been rather prone to flooding. Immediately to the north of the village, a long curving bank may be seen in the photograph, picked out by a low sun. It comes from the river at the top centre of the picture, curves around so that it almost contains the village and meets the river again near the old bridge. This is *(continued on page 35)*

References
Bu'lock 1972, 19
Lloyd 1939

Farndon

Church **NGR SJ 414544**

III 31 Farndon and Holt, looking N

Status
Farndon bridge is a Scheduled Ancient Monument

References
Jones 1991
Richards 1973, 153-6
Thacker 1987, 238-43 and 267

Photograph 31, taken in April 1977, looks north across the River Dee where it passes between Holt and Farndon. Although the two places look like two parts of the same settlement, they have always been separate. Holt is in Wales and was a medieval foundation (*see* pages 44-5), while Farndon is in Cheshire and is plainly of Dark Age origin and may be even earlier.

This photograph shows Holt on the left, with its prominent church, while Farndon is on the right, with its ancient centre at the end of the fourteenth-century bridge linking the two places.

Photograph 32, taken in May 1980, looks south-west over the bridge across the Dee. The Dark Age nature of Farndon is well illustrated in this photograph. The church, at the left of the picture, is sited on a sandstone outcrop which towers over the river. It is one of several in Cheshire which stand within a circular, or at least a curvilinear, churchyard. This is marked by a circle of trees around the church and is a sure indicator of a Dark Age foundation. Also, the church is significantly dedicated to St Chad, the Lindisfarne missionary who became bishop of the Mercian English in 669. The main street through the village is concentric with the churchyard, as can be seen, and curves sharply to meet the bridge. The photograph also shows that the line of the rock outcrop continues the curve of the road after the latter has veered to the right to cross the bridge. The rock face along the curve has plainly been trimmed at some time in the past and was possibly quarried in antiquity.

There is no record of the Dark Age church at Farndon ever having been at the centre of a monastic community. If it had been, the curved enclosed area would have contained much more than the church and churchyard. Professor G D B Jones of Manchester University has suggested that Farndon could well have been a Saxon fortified settlement. This may have been so, and would not necessarily have conflicted with the existence of an early church.

Farndon may well have been an even earlier settlement. There was certainly a Roman presence in the area, possibly in Farndon itself. Some Roman roads in the Malpas-Tilston area seem to be aligned on Farndon rather than on Chester and there may have been a river crossing here.

III 32 Farndon church and bridge, looking SW

Bangor-on-Dee *(continued from page 33)*
plainly a defensive measure against floods. There is no immediate means of ascertaining the age of the bank except possibly by an excavation or by researching local records, but it could be quite ancient. The cornfield, at the bottom right of the picture, has a similar bank curving away from the river, but this is not visible in this photograph.

Plemstall

Island home of Saxon hermit **NGR SJ 457701**

Ill 33 Plemstall church,
looking SW

References
Dodgson 1972, 135-6
Richards 1973, 273-8

Photograph 33 was taken in August 1988 looking south-west. It shows Plemstall church, which is still fairly isolated in the Gowy marshes.

The name Plemstall is a corruption of the Anglo-Saxon name *Plegmundestowe* or 'Plegmund's holy place'. Tradition has it that St Plegmund, a Mercian scholar, lived as a hermit at this spot, on the 'Island in Cheshire', in the ninth century during the troubled times of King Alfred's wars against the Danes. He became one of Alfred's chief advisers and eventually Archbishop of Canterbury. He died in 923 and was buried at Canterbury.

As the photograph shows, the 'Isle' is well named. It is a slight eminence in the once-extensive Gowy marshes. These are now low-lying meadows traversed by gutters, channels and old river courses. The River Gowy itself has been canalised and is seen crossing the picture just below the church. The isle is now roughly trapezoidal in shape, and the church with its burial ground is delineated by the edge of the platform forming the isle.

The site is very difficult to locate from the air. It is small with a group of trees, but from an aircraft, dozens of similar places with clumps of trees can be seen. It is best identified as being at the junction of the Gowy and the Chester-to-Manchester railway line which runs through Delamere. This railway crosses the photograph diagonally, above the church.

Worthenbury

Possible early fields   **NGR SJ 423488**

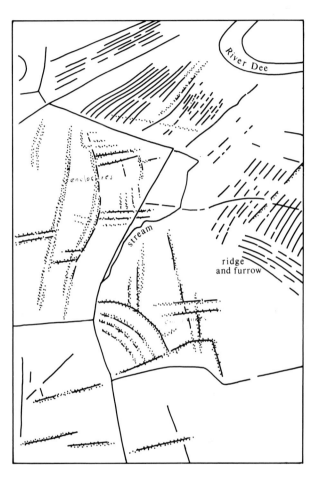

Photograph 34 was taken in August 1988, looking west across the meanders of the River Dee. Just north of this point the boundary between England and Wales leaves the River Dee and runs south-east along the Worthenbury Brook. Consequently, this site is in a kind of 'no man's land' between the Dee and Worthenbury Brook, but technically is in Wales.

The photograph shows a number of small ditches, many of them double, enclosing small areas within larger, more regular fields. Some of the areas enclosed are rectangular; others are elongated; while some of the ditches form concentric curves for no immediately obvious reason. The little enclosures are associated with traces of short lengths of ridge and furrow ploughing, some of which is straight and some curved. Some of the ridge and furrow in the area is wide and curving and medieval in appearance. Some, but by no means all of it, appears to pass over the small enclosures.

It is unlikely that the ditches were primarily field boundaries: banks would have been more appropriate. The area, lying so close to the river, is liable to flood, so the ditches can hardly have been for irrigation. The only explanation is an attempt at draining surplus water from a low-lying, frequently wet place for cultivation or pasture. One is tempted to recognise a small-scale fenland type of agriculture.

A date cannot be offered at present for these small enclosures, except to say that in size and form they are reminiscent of the small-scale fields found in Britain from the Early Iron Age, through the Roman period, to the Dark Ages.

Ills 34-5 Early fields at Worthenbury, looking W

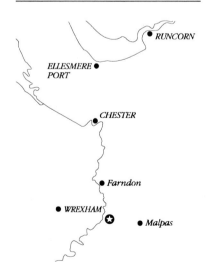

THE MEDIEVAL PERIOD

SETTLEMENTS

MOST of the medieval settlements of Cheshire still exist. With one exception, there are no large deserted villages like those of the midland counties: the settlements which have disappeared were mostly tiny hamlets. The exception is Tatton, near Knutsford, which became steadily smaller after its medieval heyday until the last few remaining cottages were swept away in the early nineteenth century to make way for the Humphrey Repton-landscaped Tatton Park we see today.

Nor were these deserted settlements all abandoned at the close of medieval times, as is often supposed. Several, whose remaining earthworks can be seen from the air, were abandoned in comparatively recent times. Such an abandonment of small settled sites does not necessarily mean that the area was depopulated and abandoned altogether. It often simply means that the pattern of landholding, and consequently of settlement, has changed somewhat since the maps were drawn or the first records were compiled.

Place-name evidence suggests that there were many small settlements, as yet unlocated, which have left no visible trace on the ground surface. One likely reason for this is that many Cheshire buildings, including churches and substantial halls, were timber-framed, and it would seem that few pre-Tudor structures in the county had stone plinths supporting the timbering. The decay of this timberwork undoubtedly led to its replacement with brick in the eighteenth century. In these circumstances, it is unlikely that timber cottages without plinths would have left any trace whatsoever, except perhaps a lane leading to them.

Several west Cheshire settlements were based upon Norman castles of the 'motte and bailey' type. These consisted of an artificial hill (the motte) which overlooked a defended courtyard (the bailey) and were the main instruments of conquest following the Norman invasion of Britain.

A small settlement was frequently created at the same time as the castle, if none already existed. There was probably a pre-Norman settlement at Aldford. Castletown in Church Shocklach, on the other hand, was probably a Norman, or near-Norman, creation, as its name implies. The castle at Malpas seems to have attracted to itself the Saxon settlement of *Depenbech*, which lay to the south-east, thereby creating the present village of Malpas.

As well as founding a settlement along with the castle, the Normans frequently created an adjacent religious foundation. There seem to be none of specifically Norman date in west Cheshire. However, it is significant that the parish churches in those west Cheshire villages which have a castle (for example, Dodleston, Pulford, Aldford, Malpas) lie within the curtilage of the former bailey. The original churches or chapels presumably served the castle's occupier and his family, the retainers and servants who lived within the bailey, and those dependants who lived outside the precincts of the castle. In later times, they became the parish churches we see today.

The medieval and immediately post-medieval character of most of Cheshire's settlements is still clearly recognisable. Some, however, were replanned in the mid-nineteenth century by improving landlords, such as the then Marquis of Westminster. Others have been expanded in recent years or have suffered from road improvements. Their original character is a little difficult to appreciate except, perhaps, with a bird's eye view from an aircraft. Such a view will invariably illustrate the old road pattern as well as several long-forgotten lanes which are now completely lost at ground level.

Malpas

Village with motte and bailey castle **NGR SJ 487472**

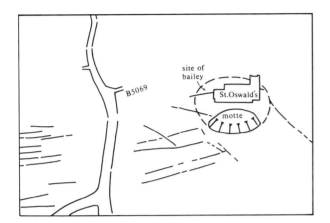

Ills 36-7 Malpas Castle and church, looking SE

Malpas derives its name from the French 'mal pas' (Latin *malus passus*) meaning 'the difficult passage'. The place was important in medieval times because of the proximity of the border with Wales. A castle, held under the Earl of Chester, was built here by Robert Fitzhugh sometime in the twelfth century. Fitzhugh played a prominent part in the Norman incursions into North Wales and was rewarded with no less than twenty-nine manors, of which Malpas was the chief.

Like most castles at that time, that at Malpas was of the motte and bailey type. Photograph 37, taken in September 1976 during the great drought, shows very clearly the motte of the castle to the right of centre of the picture. The church of St Oswald stands immediately behind it, probably on the edge of what was once the bailey of the castle. Church Street, the main east-west road running from the village cross, may be seen at the left of the photograph. This continues as the B5069 to Worthenbury and Bangor-on-Dee and represents an important route over the middle Dee to and from Wales. It is not surprising, therefore, that there was a toll passage here as well as the castle.

As mentioned above, the castle at Malpas seems to have attracted to itself settlers from the nearby Saxon village of *Depenbech*. This name has almost the same meaning as 'Malpas'. According to Dodgson, it is derived from *deopen bece*, meaning 'the place at the valley with a stream in it', presumably the difficult passage of the French name. This settlement of *Depenbech* is thought to have been at or near the Hough and the deep little valley of the Bradley Brook at Hough Bridge, 1.5 km (approximately 1 mile) south-east of Malpas.

Roman remains have been found in the Malpas area, but there is no evidence that the village existed before the Normans built their castle there. It is, however, on the line of a Roman road which came from Stretton ('Street-ton') and Tilston, and probably ultimately from Farndon and the crossing over the Dee.

Whatever the earliest history of the area may have been, the medieval village clustered about the castle, as can be seen in the photograph. The village was protected by the castle, and the castle was supported by the village.

Status
Castle Hill motte is a Scheduled Ancient Monument

References
Dodgson 1972, 38-40

Aldford

Village with motte and bailey castle   NGR SJ 419596

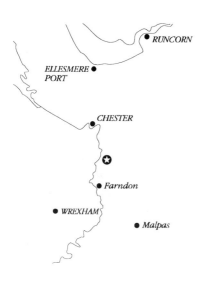

III 38 Aldford Castle, looking S

Status (Castle)
Scheduled Ancient Monument

References
Barker & Higham 1988
Dodgson 1972, 76-8
Husain 1973, 12

The Aldford that we see today owes its existence to the Normans. There had been an Anglo-Saxon interest in the area, but by the time of the Domesday Survey in 1086 it had become waste, probably as a result of the deliberate harrying of the county by William the Conqueror's armies, but possibly through Welsh raids along the border.

The Norman Aldford takes its name from an old ford near the Iron Bridge, just downstream of the village, where the Roman road, running south from Chester, crossed the Dee. This route had become disused by about 1195.

Having come as far west as the Dee, the Normans turned their attention to North Wales. In their usual fashion, they built motte and bailey castles from which they could advance further. Consequently, there is a string of such castles along the Dee, spaced a few kilometres apart. Aldford has one of these. It is 9 km from a similar castle at Church Shocklach to the south, and some 4.5 km from one at Pulford to the west. These castles along the Dee emphasise the strategic importance of the river. They also formed a barrier against any Welsh incursions towards the city of Chester.

The castle at Aldford is thought to have been built in 1276. It consisted of a motte on which there would have been a keep, probably of timber. The motte was surrounded by a wide, deep ditch which separated it from the bailey, which was itself ditched.

Photograph 38, which was taken in June 1986 looking south, shows the motte, known locally as Blobb Hill, and its surrounding ditch very clearly. It also shows the greater part of the bailey, which lies immediately above the motte in the photograph, ie between the motte and the village. The eastern, left-hand ditch of the bailey is marked by a short line of trees with long shadows, and its western ditch just touches the light-coloured yard of the farm on the right. The southern end of the bailey has long disappeared beneath the churchyard and the adjoining properties. This is a common feature of motte and bailey castles, and it can only be assumed that the church (rebuilt in 1866) stands on the site of the chapel of the castle. There would have been other buildings within the bailey. Indeed, excavations at the motte and bailey castle of Hen Domen, just outside Montgomery, have shown that a bailey could almost be choked with buildings, with little more than a passageway between them leading to the motte.

There may have been an Anglo-Saxon settlement here, but the present village seems likely to have been a Norman development, as its siting and layout

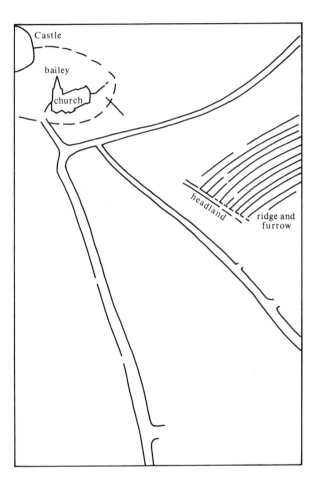

relate to the Norman motte and bailey castle. The aerial photograph shows two of the village roads or lanes pointing directly to the probable entrance into the bailey. It could be argued that the roads point towards the church, but it is more likely that the older castle governed this alignment.

Photograph 39, taken in June 1983 'looking north, shows the roads and the essential part of the village of Aldford far more clearly. The church and the castle bailey are in the top left-hand corner of the picture, and the two roads or lanes coming from the south are seen to be pointing towards the castle.

The houses in the village, with the exception of one seventeenth-century timbered building, are of Victorian date and bear witness to the extensive improvements carried out on all the Eaton estate villages by the then Marquis of Westminster.

The photograph is also interesting because the green field to the right (east) of the village has a ridge and furrow in it which, because of its curvature, is believed to be medieval. It is doubly interesting because the ridge and furrow stops on quite a prominent straight length of headland. This could well have run alongside a narrow back lane which separated the fields from the houses.

Ills 39-40 Aldford Castle bailey, church and village, looking N

Church Shocklach

Motte and bailey castle and other features at Castletown   NGR SJ 435508

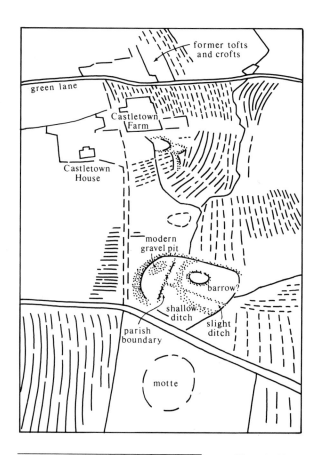

Ills 41-2 D-shaped platform at Church Shocklach, looking N E

Church Shocklach is, as its name implies, that part of the ancient parish of Shocklach where there was a church. The other two townships in the parish were Caldecott and Shocklach Oviatt. The Norman church of St Edith still stands at the head of a green lane leading down to the crossing of the River Dee about 0.5 km away. The motte and bailey castle stands about 0.5 km north of the church, at the side of the unclassified road running between Farndon and Worthenbury, near Castletown House and Castletown Farm.

Photograph 42, taken in June 1986 looking north-east, shows what was at one time thought to be the much-reduced motte of the castle. It was later thought to be the bailey, despite the raised character of the platform. The road separates it from a small wood (seen at the bottom of the picture) which conceals the real castle motte, a flat-topped conical hill or mound some four to five metres high. It is said to have been crowned with a windmill in the eighteenth/early nineteenth centuries. A stream runs through the wood, in a deep little valley, and skirts the southern (right-hand side) of the 'bailey' platform on the far side of the road.

Beyond the 'bailey' platform, ie further to the east, may be seen Castletown House. Beyond this, there is another small group of buildings which comprise Castletown Farm. This is associated with at least three slightly ditched rectangular enclosures, one of which seems to have hand-dug ridges or 'lazy beds' within it, making them look like abandoned tofts and crofts. All these buildings and features, taken together, evidently represent the ancient Castletown, a name which means 'hamlet at a castle'.

A long straight hedge can be seen running from right to left near the top of the photograph. This marks a lane, which is disused and under grass (a 'green lane') for much of its length. It runs between Lordsfields, just south of Castletown, to the vicinity of Farndon and then on to Churton. It is believed to be the

42

forerunner of the present road between Shocklach, Churton and Aldford, which includes the unclassified portion between Farndon and Worthenbury referred to above. While the green lane has all the appearance of having been a meandering medieval road, soil marks observed at one point along its length suggest it was at first a straight road of pre-medieval origin, probably Roman.

Like all motte and bailey castles, that at Church Shocklach was Norman in date and was one of a number loosely strung along the River Dee. It is thought to have been built about 1100 by a baron of Malpas. There are documentary references from about 1290 onwards to a *Castrum de Shocklach*.

The castle is believed to have guarded a route which led from a crossing over the Dee along the small deep valley of the stream into the fertile lands south of Chester. This was the route doubtless used by Welshmen from across the border, who are known to have raided the area in those times. There was also a toll gate somewhere in the vicinity of the castle, for it too was mentioned in 1290 as being at Castletown.

As has already been mentioned, the castle remains were misinterpreted until recently. The motte in the wood is now clear enough, but puzzlement still attaches to the 'bailey' platform on the east side of the road. There is no trace of a bailey attached to the motte itself. There must have been one, and the platform is the only visible candidate.

The ditch along the left (north) side of the platform is beautifully cut and follows a near-circular curve. The top of the platform is quite high above the bottom of the ditch, as well as above the road which dips down into the little valley. This apparent height above ground level probably contributed to the misinterpretation of the feature as a low motte. In contrast to this northern ditch, that on the south side rather raggedly follows the deep cut of the stream. In fact, there probably was no southern ditch as such, the deep stream bed having served as an adequate defence. It is said that the stream was originally dammed to provide water for the entire length of the ditch around the platform and that remains of this dam have been observed underneath the Farndon-Worthenbury road.

The curve of the northern ditch and the less regularly shaped stream bed combine to give the 'bailey' platform a D-shaped plan. It is not too far away from the motte to have been the bailey, or at least the eastern part of it. What connection, if any, there was between them is now difficult to determine. Possibly in the thirteenth century the site was roughly triangular or rather elongated.

There are two other possible explanations for the 'bailey' platform. The first arises out of a record that Lord Dudley petitioned King Henry VII and claimed the right to maintain the castle, fortified, ditched and crenellated. This has been interpreted by some as referring to a later and quite separate manor house on the 'bailey' platform, the original castle having been forgotten. Such a manor house may have existed on the site, but this late record hardly demonstrates that the platform was not part of the original castle complex.

The other possibility is that this D-shaped platform was, in fact, quite a separate feature from the motte and bailey castle. The platform seems to be in two parts, as may be seen in the photograph. The top right-hand quadrant seems to form a low mound which is rather separated from the rest of the structure by what seems to be a shallow, unfinished ditch. Attempts to explain the ditch as a series of shallow scoops, presumably to recover material from the mound, are not very convincing because the aerial photograph shows it to be continuous. This low separate mound has on it a small, barely discernible, banked and ditched feature forming a rather flattened circle - not quite an oval. This can only really be seen from the air with a low sun. No explanation can be offered for it at present, but it is remarkably reminiscent of a small Bronze Age disc barrow! On the left of the 'bailey' platform, there is a small but *(continued on page 46)*

(continued on page 46)

Status
Scheduled Ancient Monument

References
Dodgson 1972, 63-5
Ormerod 1882, **2**, 689
Williams 1984/5, 12

Holt

Early medieval town with castle   **NGR SJ 410538**

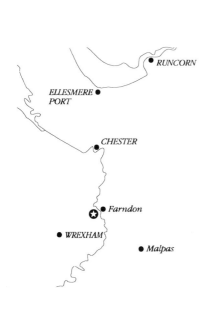

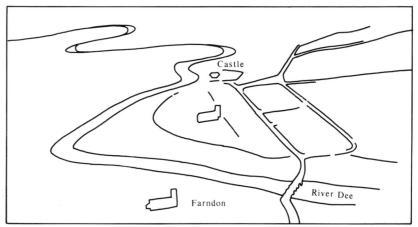

Ills 43-4 Holt under snow,
looking SW

While Holt is not in Cheshire, it is closely linked with the county because it stands on an important crossing point of the River Dee. Its history has been closely tied to that of Farndon, on the opposite bank of the river in Cheshire. Despite the geographical links between them, the origins of the two settlements are, so far as is known, quite different.

There may have been a settlement of some kind on the site of Holt before the Norman Conquest, but this is not now evident. The well known Roman tile and pottery works were only 1 km (about ½ mile) from Holt, and the river was navigable as far upstream as this. It has always been presumed that goods manufactured there, as well as other items, were shipped down-river from quays in the Holt area. There were certainly quays in the Middle Ages, so presumably in the Roman period too, although none have been identified. The mile-long stretch of river running through the low-lying land between the bridge and the vicinity of the Roman tileries is unexpectedly straight, even after allowing for the river's sudden change of course and speed caused by the sandstone bluff of Farndon. One wonders if the straightness has been emphasised and to some extent forced by the construction of quays downstream of the bridge.

It is unlikely that there was a bridge between Holt and Farndon before the thirteenth century. The river would have been forded when the water was low and perhaps crossed by boat or raft when it was in flood. It was certainly crossed,

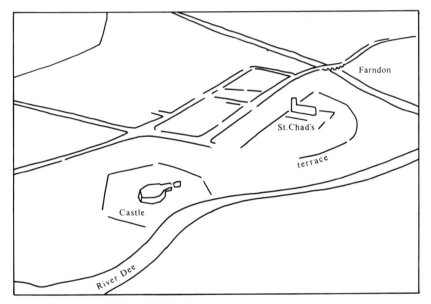

Ills 45-6 Holt Castle, looking NW

and to good effect, by Welsh drovers and traders and, in times of unrest, by raiders. This really seems to have been the *raison d'être* for the founding of Holt.

In 1282 King Edward I granted the Welsh commotes of Bromfield and Yale to John de Warenne, the Earl of Surrey, for his services in the wars against Wales. A planned town with borough status was laid out and built at Holt, which was in Bromfield. It had a church, a bridge over the Dee, and a detached tower to guard it. The castle was built sometime between 1282 and 1311, when it was first mentioned.

Photograph 43 was taken in January 1979, looking south-west. It is a view of Holt under a fall of snow, and shows the grid-iron plan along Church Street and Cross Street. The church stands out, contained within the curve of an old river terrace. In 1352 the church, or chapel as it was then, was linked with its mother church at Farndon. Not until later was it transferred to the parish of Gresford. This was not the only link between Holt and *(continued on page 46)*

References
Soulsby 1983, 144-7
Taylor 1974, 334-5
Thacker 1987, 265-6

Holt *(continued from page 45)*
Farndon, for lands in the Holt area were included, at an early date, in a large estate centred upon Farndon.

Photograph 45, taken in August 1988, shows John de Warennes's small pentagonal castle (left centre of the picture) on the river bank. To be more precise, it shows the shaped rock around which the castle was built, most of the stones having been taken away in the seventeenth century by Thomas Grosvenor to build the first Eaton Hall near Chester.

In the fourteenth century, Holt was an important town dependent largely upon agriculture and trade. As already stated, the river Dee was navigable as far as Holt, and there were important fisheries at Farndon opposite. There was also a certain amount of coal mining in the Wrexham area. Holt was one of Wales's largest boroughs, but it declined after the Black Death of 1348-9. Its decline was also hastened through being attacked by Owain Glyndwr's forces, with consequent hostility between the town's English and Welsh inhabitants.

Church Shocklach *(continued from page 43)*
deep oval pit which is relatively modern and must have been dug to recover material from the mound. At about this point, too, there is a causeway across the northern ditch. This is also probably modern, as the material in it has settled and it does not quite come up to the level of the surrounding ground. It was probably constructed to facilitate the carting of material away from the oval pit.

Taking all the evidence into consideration, it is likely that the irregular and unusual 'bailey' platform pre-dated the motte and bailey castle. What use was made of it during the castle's occupation is unknown. Its form does not suggest it was a Roman feature, but it may well have been a prehistoric one - quite possibly with a religious function.

There are a number of other slight features which have been formed on the platform through the years. The most prominent is a straight shallow ditch running east, which marks the civil parish boundary between Church Shocklach and Caldecott.

It is alleged that a great deal of damage has been done to the castle site during this century through attempts to level the land for agriculture. The aerial photograph suggests that this has been greatly exaggerated and was probably confined to little more than digging the oval pit and building the small causeway. Ormerod wrote that the platform had 'been levelled in part for the purposes of making a garden'. The effect of this also seems to have been exaggerated. Interestingly, he doubted if this platform had ever been part of the castle and suggested it was part of an ancient work protecting the Roman Watling Street.

Dodleston

Village with motte and bailey castle **NGR SJ 361608**

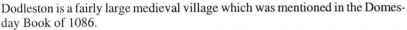

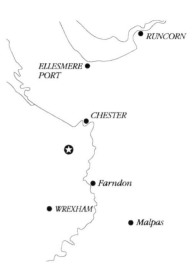

III 47 Dodleston, looking NE

Dodleston is a fairly large medieval village which was mentioned in the Domesday Book of 1086.

The photograph, taken in March 1982 looking north-east, shows the main elements on which the village was based. The circular wooded area at the bottom centre contains what remains of the motte and bailey castle, believed to have been built in the reign of King Richard I (1189-99). It is one of the string of minor castles strategically placed between the Welsh border and Chester. This castle and the similar one at Pulford were on the west side of the Dee, ie beyond the natural boundary between England and Wales. Evidently the barons considered such outposts to be essential in a marshy terrain which must have been difficult to control. The large house within the circular area is the Old Rectory. This occupies the motte, while the bailey takes up the rest of the circle.

Immediately beyond the castle, on the very edge of the circular area, may be seen the church of St Mary, which was given to the abbot and convent of St Werburgh, Chester about the time of King John (1199-1216) by Alan de Boydell, who held the lordship of Dodleston from the Earl of Chester. This is another example of a parish church sited immediately adjacent to the bailey of a castle. As previously mentioned, it and similarly placed churches were presumably first founded as chapels for the use of the castle's occupiers and their immediate dependants.

The village is a little unusual, but not unique, in having a pre-eminent building, ie a hall, as well as a castle. Presumably the castle site had lost its importance when the hall was built. It is not known when this was, but in 1393 it was the home of one Robert del Hall. The hall stood within a large moated area, but it has since been replaced by a Georgian farmhouse, also called the Hall, and other buildings, on an adjoining site. The large moated area is still visible but the moat ditch has silted up.

Dodleston has, unhappily, lost much of its medieval character. Most of the timber-built cottages were replaced by solid, practical, brick houses in the mid-nineteenth century. Much of the road layout was also altered about that time. Some have been re-aligned while others, notably near the church, have disappeared completely. One road, retained as a hollow way, came down from the north towards the church, presumably originally to the castle. This has disappeared in recent years under new housing development, although attempts were made to retain portions of it as a feature in the gardens of the new houses.

Status (Castle)
Scheduled Ancient Monument

References
Dodgson 1972, 156-7

Ince

Monastic grange   NGR SJ 449765

III 48 Ince Manor and Monastery
Cottages, looking SE

Status
(Manor and cottages)
Buildings of Special Architectural
Interest
(Rectangular area)
Scheduled Ancient Monument

References
Davey & Williams 1975

The site of the grange now known as Ince Manor occupies the prominent rectangle in the centre of the photograph, taken in February 1983. A grange was a monastic farm, and this one belonged to the Benedictine abbey of St Werburgh at Chester. Its history is fully documented from its Anglo-Saxon origins to the fifteenth century, when it was included with the other properties of St Werburgh in the endowment of the new cathedral at Chester. King Edward I stayed here in August 1277 after travelling from Birkenhead Priory and laying the foundation stone of Vale Royal Abbey.

The photograph shows two of the grange's major buildings, which are still substantially complete. One, the wide building with the brightly reflecting roof at the side of the road (Marsh Lane), is known as the Manor and was probably the guest hall of the establishment. It dates to the fifteenth century. The roofless building along the bottom of the rectangle, known as Monastery Cottages, was the domestic range. Architectural details suggest that it dates to the late thirteenth or early fourteenth century. There is evidence that a third building occupied part of the right-hand side of the rectangle. Other buildings outside the rectangle incorporate medieval stonework and may represent for-mer barns and so on, while the lengths of moulded stonework along Kinsey's Lane, on the right of the picture, suggest estate walls.

Caldecott Green

Diminished or shrunken settlement   **NGR SJ 429520**

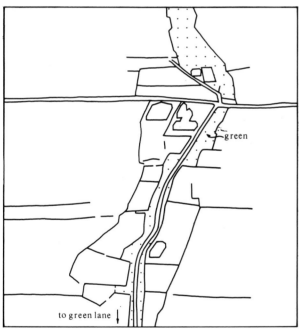

Caldecott, one of the three townships of Shocklach, was mentioned in the Domesday Survey of 1086. According to Dodgson, the name is a common one in England and, in his opinion, refers to temporary dwellings which would not have been heated (ie, cold cotts). Presumably, Dodgson meant that they would not have been provided with internal hearths.

Photograph 49 was taken in 1976 during the great drought. The photograph, looking west, shows Caldecott Green as a linear village with the remnants of a strip green appearing as a wide irregular verge on both sides of the lane leading through it. There are several small enclosed areas, some of which still retain buildings, while others are now empty of any structures. Some of these will have been paddocks and crofts, but some will once have contained farmhouses or cottages. *(Continued on page 51)*

Ills 49-50 Caldecott shrunken settlement, looking W

References
Dodgson 1972, 62

Bruera

Diminished or shrunken settlement   **NGR SJ 437606**

Ills 51-2 Bruera shrunken settlement, looking W

Status
The moated site and adjacent field system are Scheduled Ancient Monuments

References
Dodgson 1972, 115-16
Richards 1973, 70-4

This aerial photograph, taken in June 1986 looking west, shows several ancient features. Most prominent is the square moated site in the centre of the photograph. Three of its ditches remain but are now silted up and dry, while the fourth ditch, completing the square, now lies largely beneath the road running from right to left (Chapel Lane). The road from the bottom centre of the photograph now comes from the A41 trunk road, but it is probably aligned on the original lane leading to the entrance to the moated site. The building now within the moated area is an eighteenth/nineteenth-century farmhouse and probably bears no relation to whatever originally occupied the site. As the site was moated, this is likely to have been a house but not necessarily so. That the moat was of medieval date can be demonstrated by the ridge and furrow of medieval character which comes up to it but does not encroach upon it in any way.

To the left (south) of the moated site, surrounded by trees, can be seen the little church of St Mary. This was built in the twelfth century and some original work remains, although it was extensively restored in 1896. It may have been in existence when the moated site was created.

Immediately opposite the right-hand corner of the moat, across the road, three or four small ditched enclosures are visible. These have recently been claimed as former paddocks, but they are just as likely to have been the sites of cottages, not necessarily very ancient.

A long straight hedge can be seen coming up from near the bottom left-hand corner of the picture. It continues, with a break near the centre, to the wood at the top right-hand corner. This hedge is partly followed by a hollow way and, where the break in the hedge occurs, there is clearly disturbed ground where dwellings formerly stood. These, and the road which is now a hollow way, are shown on a map of Aldford parish published in 1839.

The evidence from aerial photography, old maps and so on shows that Bruera is a shrunken or diminished settlement. Whether it should be regarded as a shrunken medieval one is a little more problematical.

Problems of identification and interpretation have arisen out of a confusion of parish and township here. Originally, Bruera (which seems to be derived from Low Latin for 'a heath') was a chapelry of St Oswald's parish, Chester. It is also referred to as Churton Heath (derived from 'Church-on-heath', not to be confused with Churton-by-Farndon).

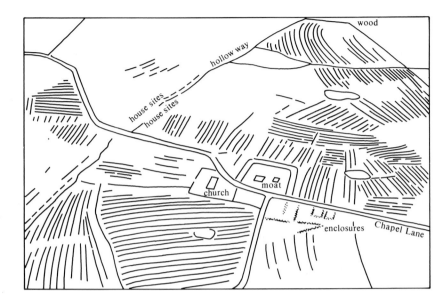

A parish boundary passes along Chapel Lane, separating the church from the moat, leaving the former in Bruera, or Churton Heath, and the latter in Buerton, a township of Aldford parish. Similarly, the hollow way and cottages, still extant in 1839, were technically in Buerton township. This would seem to be a rather ridiculous situation, as the place was plainly one settlement in fairly recent times if not in the Middle Ages.

A lot has been written about the chapel at Bruera which gave its name to Chapel Lane and to Chapelhouse Farm. Much of this seems logical in relation to the various parish boundaries but is very confusing regarding the chapel. It has been claimed that the chapel was in Saighton but gave its name to Churton Heath (as above). It has also been claimed that, while the chapel was in Saighton, it may have had a more ancient location at Bruera, the moated site being suggested.

It would seem to be far more sensible to concede that the chapel at Bruera, referred to in 1141 and later as *Ecclesia Sancte Marie de Bruera*, and the *Capella de Bouwario* of AD 1216 and later, must surely be one and the same as the Norman church of St Mary which still stands, albeit much restored, a matter of yards from the medieval moated site. The church is in fact shown and labelled 'chapel' on the map of Aldford parish drawn in 1839 and referred to earlier.

Despite the late date of some of the former house sites and so on, it can be argued that there was a small settlement at Bruera in the Middle Ages. This partly consisted of a chapel, a moated house and a number of cottages.

Caldecott Green *(continued from page 49)*

The eastern end of the lane through the village joins the green lane (ie, an abandoned road) that still runs from Churton in the north down to Lordsfields in Church Shocklach. As is typical of most medieval settlements in Cheshire, there is a hall, or pre-eminent house, sited just a little way outside the village. This is Caldecott Hall, 0.25 km to the south, which is also linked to the green lane. That the village had diminished some time ago is borne out by the tithe award map of 1841, which shows the place more or less as it is today. However, one or two buildings have disappeared since then, showing that the process is still continuing slowly.

Overton

Small deserted settlement   **NGR SJ 474483**

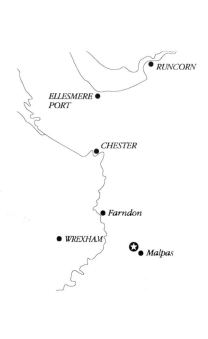

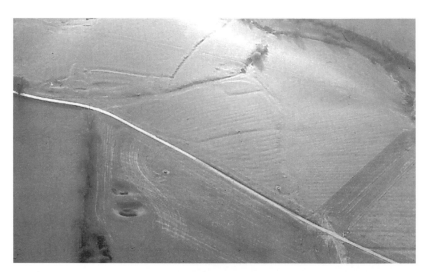

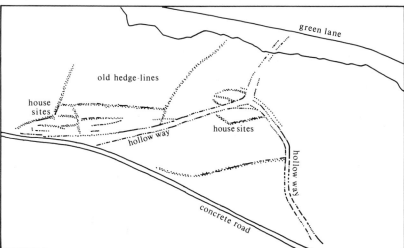

Ills 53-4 Overton deserted
settlement, looking S

References
Burdett 1777, viii
Dodgson 1972, 45

Overton, a township of Malpas parish, was mentioned in the Domesday Survey under the name *Overtone*. The name has been perpetuated in Overton Hall, Overton Scar and Overton Heath. Burdett's map of Cheshire, published in 1777, shows an Overton Green as well.

The place was commonly called 'Ourton' in the seventeenth century. This explains the Welsh name 'Wrtyn' for the other Overton (ie, on Dee). The area is now one of scattered farms. That the settlement once consisted of buildings much closer together, near to the hall, is shown in Ill 53. This shows several earthworks and a complex of lanes, all indicative of a formerly inhabited site.

A hollow way may be seen running up from near the bottom right-hand corner to near the centre of the photograph, where it forms a T-junction with another hollow way. Slight ditches associated with formerly existing buildings can be seen at this junction. The second hollow way runs towards the top of the photograph, where it meets a green lane with rather straggling hedges. In the other direction, it runs towards the left of the photograph, where it meets the modern concrete farm road. Near this junction the disturbed ground of other house sites may be seen.

The site is one of west Cheshire's few visible deserted settlements. It does not, however, represent a medieval deserted village. The tithe award map of 1840 shows at least ten structures within the area of the photograph.

Chowley

Deserted hamlet　**NGR SJ 477563**

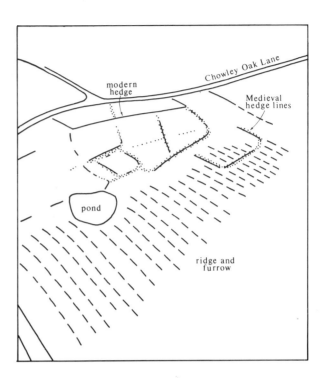

Ills 55-6 Chowley deserted hamlet, looking W

Chowley was an early settlement mentioned in the Domesday Survey of 1086 under the spelling *Celelea*, meaning 'Ceola's wood or clearing' according to Dodgson. It is one of those curious places which has been deserted and re-occupied only fairly recently when a large farmhouse and a terrace of cottages was built. The latter are still occupied but the farmhouse has been demolished. Photograph 55, taken in 1986 looking west, shows the farmhouse, and the terrace of cottages is at the top left.

The present unclassified road (Chowley Oak Lane), running from right to left at the top of the picture, cuts through the remains of the medieval hamlet. These appear as a series of small, shallow-ditched enclosures with long post-medieval ridge and furrow coming up to them. A round pond of recent date has been cut through the ridge and furrow and is right at the edge of the settled area.

It is not known when the enclosed areas (tofts and crofts) were abandoned. The post-medieval ridge and furrow stops short of all but one of them, which suggests they were abandoned during that period, possibly in Tudor or Stuart times. No trace of the settlement can now be seen on the other (west) side of Chowley Oak Lane. No doubt any·surviving traces were obliterated by the newer buildings and by the construction of the now abandoned Chester to Whitchurch railway line.

A holy well and a 'Holy Well Chapel', mentioned in 1533, seem to have been associated with the township rather than with the hamlet. They were presumably sited at Holywell, about 1 km to the south. There is now no trace of them.

References
Dodgson 1972, 84

Hetherson Green

Diminished or shrunken settlement   NGR SJ **528495** (centre of village)

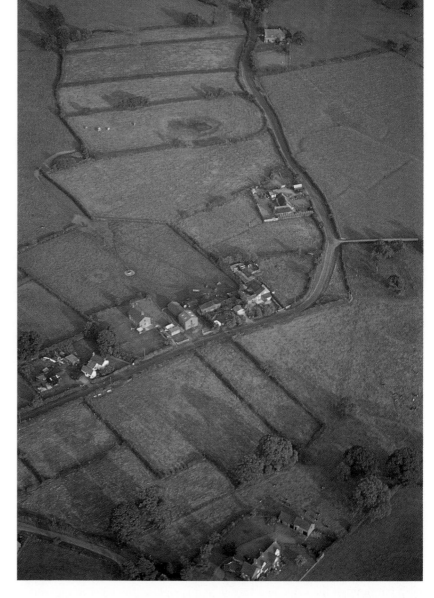

Ill 57 Hetherson Green diminished settlement, looking S

References
Dodgson 1972, 8-9
Williams 1984/5, 12

Hetherson Green is a village in the Bickley township of Malpas parish. Its name at present defies interpretation and has, in any case, varied through the years. In 1506 it was referred to as Hetheston; as Heleston in 1540; Hethe-housey Green in 1705; and Edwardson Green in 1860.

The aerial photograph was taken in mid-July 1989 looking south and shows the central part of the village. It also illustrates its two main characteristics. The first is that the settlement is now a strung-out linear one on a lane which has a sharp bend. This sharp bend, at the centre of the village, is due to its having developed along one side of a curious network of lanes lying between Bickley, Edgerton and Cholmondeley. The other characteristic is that there is a large number of empty enclosures along the village street or lane. These enclosures cannot all have been paddocks or cultivated crofts. *(Continued on page 56)*

Spurstow

Possible small deserted settlement at Haycroft Farm   **NGR SJ 554573**

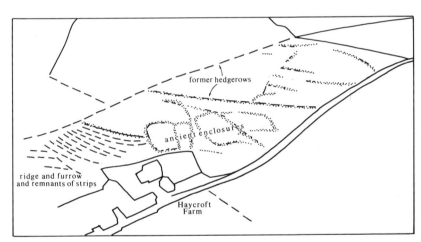

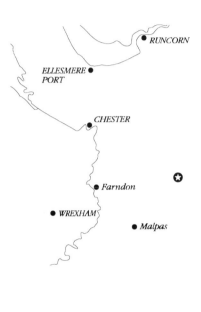

Ills 58-9 Haycroft Farm, looking E

Spurstow, in the parish of Bunbury, was mentioned in the Domesday Survey and the settlement may be older than that. It is near a Roman route between Tarporley and Whitchurch and near an old salt route between Nantwich and the crossing over the Dee at Farndon. There were also saline springs (Spurstow Spa) some 3 km (2 miles) to the south-east.

Haycroft Farm stands about 0.5 km (¼ mile) west of Spurstow on the old track which once led to the Peckforton Hills and to Beeston Moss. The name 'Haycroft' suggests farming rather than a settlement. However, the present farm-house is the successor to an earlier house which stood with other small buildings at this spot. These are all shown on an eighteenth-century map of the area. The name was, perhaps, one given to the house, and may have had nothing to do with the former use of the piece of land on which it was built.

The aerial photograph (Ill 58), taken in June 1979 looking east, shows Haycroft Farm and the associated fields. The hedges of some of these fields have been taken up in recent years, but their lines can still be clearly seen. Underlying these fields may be seen a string of small roughly rectangular enclosures which run away from the road to behind the farm buildings. While the ground in this area is a little hummocky, this cannot account for the fairly regular rectangular shape and consistent size of the ditched features. Nor can it be argued that the narrow ditches themselves are merely products of water erosion. The features look very much like small crofts *(continued on page 56)*

Hetherson Green (*continued from page 54*)
Some must have been tofts, ie, house plots. Most of the enclosures are still hedged about. Others have had their hedges removed but are still recognisable by the shallow ditches which ran alongside the hedges. Some of these former enclosures can be seen in the right centre of the photograph.

From an archaeological viewpoint there are two areas, one to the west and one to the south of the existing village, which have features revealed by a low sun. These features comprise boundary ditches as mentioned above, a possible hollow way and old marl pits, ponds and so on. These are plainly of varying date. Some are cut through ridge and furrow plough marks, while others contain small parcels of it. A few of the features appear as hedge lines on late nineteenth- and early twentieth-century maps, but most of them do not.

All these features and the many surviving small hedged enclosures fronting onto both sides of the lane suggest that Hetherson Green was not always a linear village but is a shrunken nucleated one and that there may once have been a continuation of the village as a ribbon development to the south. The wide verge at the sharp bend in the lane hints at a former village green.

A second area of wide verges occurs at and near the junction of the village street or lane with Grotsworth Lane. This could be the remnant of another small green. It is possible that the settlement may have moved northwards from here to its present centre. Alternatively, the present Hetherson Green could have evolved out of an early polyfocal settlement, the southern element of which has now been largely lost. Hetherson Green is a most interesting settlement which would repay further study and research.

Spurstow (*continued from page 55*)
or even tofts and crofts which once fronted onto a lane or perhaps a small green where Haycroft Farm now stands. It is also probably significant that a wide curving ridge and furrow (ie, medieval type) runs up to the low enclosures but does not pass over them.

No name can be offered for this habitation site. The site has a clay soil, while Spurstow itself is on rather sandy ground. The clay does not preclude settlement, although it would not have been the settlers' first choice. It is suggested that the site at Haycroft Farm represents an attempt by the people of Spurstow to expand their village a little and colonise some of the rich land round about. It may be that this long-forgotten act took place in the thirteenth century but had to be abandoned after a short while, possibly following the decimation of families by the Black Death or because of worsening weather conditions and rising water tables, which also occurred at that time.

A moated site consists of a platform and ditches which were usually filled with water. These ditches need not necessarily surround the platform on all sides, and moats with three arms, or even with two arms forming an angle, can be found. Whether some of these are unfinished examples is not known. Moats are sometimes double, having ditches encompassing other ditches. In some cases, these may be due to refortification or strengthening of simple domestic moats during the Civil War.

Moats may be linked to watercourses or to a system of ditches. Somewhere in their vicinity there may be old fishponds or a mill pool, now probably dry but recognisable by their man-made appearance. Although these were associated with the moated site, they can seem to be independent of it in that they may be some distance away.

In addition to these variations, multiple moats consisting of two or more rectangles grouped together are not uncommon. The principal moat could well have contained a house and the others could have been pounds or served some other non-domestic purpose.

The platform or island contained by the moat ditches need not be a rectangle. Moated areas can have a rounded end, or form a trapezium or exceptionally be circular. Nor is the platform always at one level, although it usually is. Several platforms have an uneven surface, suggesting the presence of foundation walls or building debris beneath the turf. It is noticeable that the surface of the platform is in many cases considerably higher than the ground surface outside the moat. There are two possible explanations for this. Firstly, material from excavating the moat ditches may have been spread over the platform and consolidated before anything was built on it. Secondly, it may be the result of very long occupation of the site, with soils and debris having accumulated and been levelled in the course of time.

Archaeological excavations and documentary research show that moated sites are usually of medieval date, beginning in the twelfth century, rising to a peak in the mid-thirteenth to the mid-fourteenth centuries and diminishing in the sixteenth century and later (Aberg ed 1978, 27). Most of them contained houses and other structures; some moated sites still do so. Little Moreton Hall is a very well known Cheshire example; Chorley Old Hall, near Alderley Edge, is a less well known but very important example.

Moats did not always surround houses, however. They are known to have contained orchards and gardens, even haystacks, and some may have been pounds. However, their main function seems to have been to separate a house of some importance from the landscape in which it stood.

At the last count 180 moats had been recorded in Cheshire. Most of them were abandoned long ago and are now represented only by shallow, silted-up ditches. They may stand alone in fields or adjoin farmhouses which often bear the significant name 'Hall'. They often have later hedgerows passing over them without any recognition of their former status and importance. Some moats are now only visible as cropmarks, in grass or growing cereals, during rather exceptional seasons of drought such as the summer of 1976. Yet other moats have left no trace but are sometimes shown on early nineteenth-century maps of rural parishes.

In Cheshire, most if not all moated sites contained a house of some importance: perhaps a manor house or a monastic grange, or even the simpler, but still superior, hall of a yeoman farmer.

6

THE MEDIEVAL PERIOD

MOATED SITES

There was usually no more than one family in a township, or even in a parish, sufficiently important to have a moated house. Moats in Cheshire, therefore, tend to occur on the basis of no more than one per township or, more likely in some areas, one per parish. There seem to be very few exceptions to this. This does not mean, of course, that there was a moated house somewhere in each parish. There are areas of the county where there are none or, at least, very few. The moated site in Cheshire is essentially a lowland feature. There are none on the foothills of the Pennines in the east and few on the sandy soils of the south-east. They are conspicuously absent from the forest area of Mare and Mondrum (now Delamere Forest), and only two (Irby and Bromborough) are known on the sandstone peninsula of Wirral. In contrast, there are many moats on the clay soils around Chester and Nantwich, but again with a distribution of no more than one per township. Both Chester and Nantwich were important places in the Middle Ages, and a number of comparatively wealthy people could be expected in these areas.

Moated houses tend to fall into one of two categories so far as they relate to villages or other settlements. Those that belonged to important, well established families tended to be isolated, within their own estates, and be rather removed from the communities to which they were otherwise linked. The town of Knutsford, for example, is ringed with such estates, each with its own hall. Three of the four moated sites illustrated here, namely those at Foulk Stapleford (Ill 60), Rake Lane, Eccleston (Ills 61-2) and Belgrave (Ill 63), while not halls of the first rank, seem to fall into this category.

The most important moated houses would have been self-contained and self-sufficient to a large extent. Each house would have consisted of an open great hall, with a solar or private chamber over part of it, and a kitchen with ancillary stores. There would probably have been a chapel, bakehouse, brewhouse, stables, a barn and perhaps a dovecote. An orchard or a garden could also have been included within the moated area, which was usually large, and there would have been fishponds just outside. There could also have been ancillary structures outside the moat as well as various paddocks and so on.

The large houses called halls that we see within, or just on the edge of, many villages, belong to the second category of moated sites. They are generally held to have been those of less important, though locally eminent, families: that is, they were people who, despite their position, were far more dependent upon the community than were their wealthier counterparts. However, a note of caution must be sounded here. As explained below, many halls and other locally important houses had been sited upon rather poor, damp clay ground. Furthermore, the great house would largely have been built of timber which had a limited life. During the Tudor and following periods, great houses built on such sites became very unfashionable. To say the least, they were draughty, damp and in constant need of repair. The sites were therefore frequently abandoned and the family moved to a better-built brick or stone house sited on higher ground much nearer to the village, leaving the old moated site, on low ground, to become silted up and forgotten. It is unwise, therefore, to try to classify halls by their location alone. The date of the building and much else should be taken into account.

The damp clay soils on which very many of the moated houses of Cheshire were located are likely to have been wooded. Indeed, such moated sites have been regarded by some as the very nuclei from which a systematic process of woodland clearance was carried out. This introduces several other facets of Cheshire moats and perhaps of moats everywhere.

Firstly, the purpose of a moat is not now held to have been defensive in the military sense. The dimensions of a domestic moat ditch, though in some cases over 50 feet in width (Moated Sites Research Group Report No 11, 1984, 5 -7) in east Cheshire, would hardly have stopped a determined army onslaught as doubtless witnessed by many a Cheshire great house during the Civil War. The moats around castles, such as Beaumaris in Anglesey, or fortified manor houses, such as Stokesay in Shropshire, are in a very different category and were designed to withstand such an onslaught.

On the other hand, there is a slight defensive element involved. In east Cheshire, for example, it is said that several of the landed families were involved in feuds. It seems that the moats around their houses played much the same part as the defensive domestic towers so well known in medieval Italy. Moats must also have formed a defence against animals. As has already been said, most of them are likely to have been in close proximity to woodland. Such a setting could have meant predatory wolves and browsing deer, if nothing else. The New Pale, in Delamere, was a large enclosure created in the reign of Charles II for the 'protection of vert (ie, vegetation) and venison'. The vert usually needed protection from the venison, and no doubt moats played their part in doing this at the domestic level.

Secondly, the situation of many moated houses on low-lying damp clay soils suggests that the ditch served as a drain for surface water, the fall of the ground hopefully enabling the water to run away from the house.

Because of their situation on low ground, there rarely seems to have been a need to bring water into the ditch by diverting a stream or creating a channel to collect extra rainwater: the site was so low-lying that ground water simply welled up in the ditch. The problem was not so much to bring water in as to get rid of excess. Most moats in west Cheshire, therefore, had some sort of sluice gate arrangement by which water could be let out into a run-off channel leading to the nearest ditch or anything else that would take it away. The site at Rake Lane, Eccleston (Ills 61-2) shows the positions of both of these very clearly.

The need to regulate the water level was matched by the need to empty the moat completely at times. Ditches naturally become silted up and occasionally needed re-cutting. Also it must be remembered that the ditch was probably an all-too-obvious place into which to throw domestic rubbish. (It is also interesting to speculate how many stone-built drains leading from a house into a moat have given rise to legends of escape tunnels and secret passages). And so the moat ditch occasionally had to be cleared of rubbish. As a result, archaeologists usually find moat ditches rather unrewarding places to excavate. There are never very many finds in them, and in consequence the dates of their first cutting and subsequent re-cutting are not at all easy to determine.

No doubt in the course of time the moat came to be seen more and more as a status symbol. If the baron in his castle could have a moat, why could not the yeoman have one for his house? Few surviving moats in west Cheshire have become ornamental as one or two in the east of the county have become. The fourteenth-century Chorley Old Hall, near Alderley Edge, has a terrace which looks towards a little waterfall where the old sluice gate once stood and exotic waterfowl paddle lazily among clumps of ornamental reeds. The hall is approached over a fine double-arched sixteenth-century bridge. Such access bridges are rare in the west of the county: at least, few have survived. There is one very good bridge at Lower Huxley Hall and another at Hulme Hall, Allastock. Almost every one of the moated sites in the west of the county seems to have had access across a wooden bridge (*see* Ills 61-2) or over a causeway.

Moats generally in west Cheshire seem to have been 'working moats', if that is an apt expression; few seem to have become status symbols. When they no longer fulfilled their function, most of them were apparently just ignored and left to silt up. Several of them have been filled in in recent years, but most are now protected by being scheduled as Ancient Monuments.

Foulk Stapleford

Moated site on the River Gowy   **NGR SJ 484641**

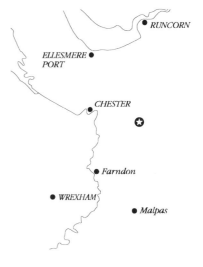

III 60 Foulk Stapleford moated site, looking N

The aerial photograph, taken from the south with a low sun in February 1983, shows a sub-rectangular moat on the banks of the now canalised River Gowy. The river formerly meandered quite considerably northwards towards the Gowy marshes, and traces of several former minor channels may be seen in the vicinity of the moated site.

A little way to the right (north-east) of the moat, a small straight-sided depression with curved ends may be seen. It is parallel to the northern ditch of the moat and apparently relates to it. It may have been a small fishpond, although the feature seems to be a little too small for that purpose.

The moat was presumably the site of a hall. Its location just within the boundary of Foulk Stapleford township (now a parish) suggests that there may have been a Foulk Stapleford Hall, as well as a Stapleford Hall in the adjoining township of Bruen Stapleford (also now a parish). This latter hall still exists some 0.75 km to the east of the moated site.

According to Dodgson, the manor of Stapleford was undivided before 1243. The moated site may belong to this period, with Stapleford Hall originating after the division into two townships. There is another possibility. As previously said, during the seventeenth and eighteenth centuries the old timber-framed halls on low ground frequently gave way to structures built of more durable materials on better sites . The present Stapleford Hall could conceivably be the successor to a much older one located within the moat.

Status
Scheduled Ancient Monument

References
Dodgson 1971, 269-70

Eccleston

Moated site at Rake Lane   NGR SJ 401626

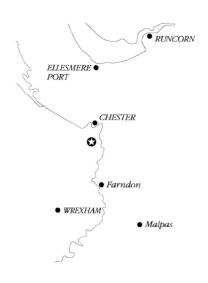

Ills 61-2 Eccleston Rake Lane
moated site, looking N

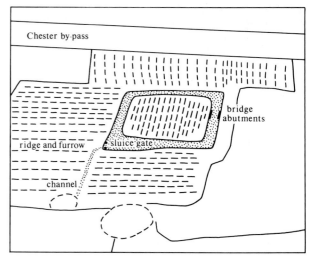

This moated enclosure (Ill 61) stands between Rake Lane and the Chester southerly by-pass, which is shown in the photograph. It is not known what the moat enclosed, but all the evidence points to a house or hall as yet unidentified. The area contained by the moat is rectangular with slightly rounded corners. Examination on the ground reveals that the ditch is now quite shallow, having at some time been filled in or allowed gradually to silt up almost completely. The latter is the more likely, as the ridge and furrow which has been ploughed within the moated area after it was abandoned does not maintain the direction of the ridge and furrow on either side of it, ie the ditch at that time was still a barrier to ploughing.

The aerial photograph, which was taken in 1977, is unusual in that it shows the moat ditch filled, not with water, but with ice, which appears black from the air. The photograph is also instructive in that two features not normally seen at this site are made clearly visible by the varying thickness of the ice. It is a little thinner, and consequently appears grey, on both banks of the moat ditch at a point halfway along the right (eastern) side of the moated area. This clearly marks the abutments of a formerly existing bridge, ie the entrance to the ☞

Status
Scheduled Ancient Monument

Eccleston (Eaton Park)

Moat at Belgrave Moat Farm   **NGR SJ 390605**

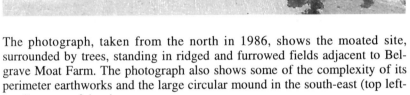

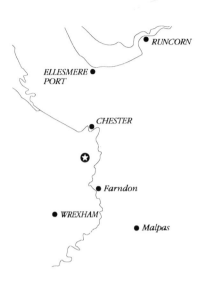

Ill 63 Eccleston Belgrave Moat Farm moated site, looking SE

The photograph, taken from the north in 1986, shows the moated site, surrounded by trees, standing in ridged and furrowed fields adjacent to Belgrave Moat Farm. The photograph also shows some of the complexity of its perimeter earthworks and the large circular mound in the south-east (top left-hand) corner of the site.

A small manor existed here from the 1280s and is known from documentary evidence to have been the property of Richard the Engineer, one of Edward I's military architects. He was especially concerned with the building of Flint Castle, together with its fortified town, between 1277 and 1286. The first mention of a house at Belgrave was in 1309, when Richard divided his rural holdings amongst his family, the property at Belgrave being rented to his son for £10 *per annum*. It is thought that the site was abandoned as a residence as early as the end of the fourteenth century and then used for coppiced woodland.

It had long been assumed that there was a village or hamlet of Belgrave, which gave its name to Belgravia (the well known Grosvenor estate in London) but all efforts by archaeologists and others to find it have ended in failure. Contemporary records place Belgrave in the township of *Eaton-boate*, which also cannot now be located. The *-boate* suffix suggests that any settlement of that name would be on the banks of the River Dee, where there would have been a ferry boat. Belgrave, however, is 3 km (nearly 2 miles) from the river and nowhere near such a settlement. It is thought likely that the Belgrave moated site is an example of a self-contained residence or hall not closely dependent upon, nor immediately adjacent to, a village or other settlement.

It has yet to be proved by archaeological excavation that the moated site did contain a house. Although it must surely have done so in this case, moats did not always surround houses. The moat sometimes protected something that the owner valued more highly than even his dwelling, especially if it was not his main dwelling. Richard the Engineer's main house *(continued on page 65)*

Status
Scheduled Ancient Monument

☞site. Similarly, there are two blobs of grey ice at the bottom left-hand (south-west) corner of the moat. These are clearly the settings for the posts of a sluice gate, which would have connected the moat to a water run-off channel linking it to a nearby stream or ditch. The line of this channel is emphasised in the photograph by a slight shadow and a corresponding highlight.

Hampton

Features at Hampton Grange

Ills 64-5 Features at Hampton Grange

Hampton is an ancient place-name which is recorded in the Domesday Survey as *Hantone*. It is one of twenty-four townships within the ancient ecclesiastical parish of Malpas. The name has rarely appeared by itself, usually being accompanied by a descriptive appellation giving Hampton Croft, Grange, Green, Hall, Heath, Old Hall and Hampton Post. Most of these names are self-explanatory and describe features or local places which still exist, for example Hampton Green and Hampton Hall.

The name Hampton Grange is a little puzzling. In Cheshire, it usually refers to a farm complex owned by a religious house. For example the abbeys of St Werburgh and Vale Royal had five granges, and Combermere Abbey, southwest of Nantwich, had three. A grange at Hampton does not seem to be mentioned amongst the properties of these great houses, but it may have been a secular establishment and the home of a local gentleman farmer. The name now applies particularly to the farm shown in Ill 64, which was taken with a very low sun in August 1976.

Curiously no field name such as 'grange field' or 'grange croft' seems to have survived at this spot, as might have been expected with an ancient site. On the other hand, the photograph shows several low earthworks which are quite invisible from the air in normal daylight. They are plainly older than the present farm buildings and could be of considerable antiquity.

Immediately below the farm buildings in the photograph there is a right-angled ditch which is probably shallow but is thrown into sharp relief by the low sun. The ditch seems far too slight to have been that of a moat and was probably just a ditch which ran along two sides of a small field whose hedges have long since vanished.

Residual short lengths of ridge and furrow ploughing can be seen in the photograph between this small enclosure and the farm buildings. This ridge and furrow is of a curving variety, suggesting a medieval or sixteenth/seventeenth century date at the latest. It stops at the ditch and is presumably contemporary with it. Its orientation would have taken it under the present farm buildings which have apparently been built over it on what had been cultivated ground, so the buildings can hardly be on the site of any original grange buildings.

To the left of the farm buildings, there is a complex of very low mounds and one or two wide but shallow ditch-like areas which, once again, are accentuated by the low sun. The photograph also shows a slightly sunken track running

References
Sylvester & Nulty eds 1958, 24-5

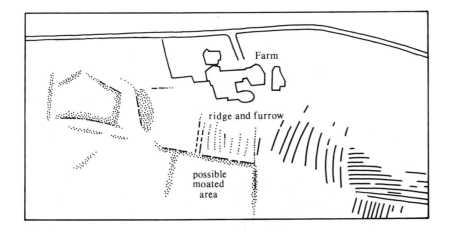

from the earthworks to the present complex of buildings. The mounds themselves incorporate a right angle, which might suggest a much-altered moat. This interpretation is not, however, very convincing, and any resemblance to the outlines of an ancient moat is superficial and must be due to pure chance. The low mounds may, in fact, be purely geological in origin which, in a county of sands and clays like Cheshire, is always a possibility. Against this, ridge and furrow ploughing has not been extended over these earthworks as it has over low natural mounds at other sites in the county. But it would have stopped short of any buildings or moat at this spot.

The most likely explanation is that the low earthworks are the result of human activity and disturbance of one kind or another. They may well have been associated with a house that predated the present farm complex - possibly the original Hampton Grange.

Eccleston (Eaton Park) *(continued from page 63)*
was at Chester, in what is now Lower Bridge Street. He was a prominent citizen, and it was here rather than at Belgrave that he had business interests quite unconnected with his work for Edward I.

An exhaustive survey and a limited archaeological excavation during 1985/ 6 by Cheshire County Council produced some interesting and unexpected results. The moat's earthworks proved to be more complex than was expected. According to the archaeologists' survey report, 'the moat was trapezoidal and enclosed a platform 6,750 square metres in area'. Unusually, there were lesser earthworks surrounding the main ditch on three sides, while the north-west corner was dominated by a nearly circular, flat-topped mound 1.8 m high. The archaeologists concluded that 'the earthworks around the three sides of the moated platform ...... represented the structure of a garden'. Lawns and herb gardens are known from this period (ie, the thirteenth/fourteenth centuries) and they were even associated with castles in military zones, such as Conwy and Caernarfon in North Wales.

The archaeologists' report also speculates that 'if the ditches at the Belgrave moat are imagined as walls, it makes a most convincing castle'. The report goes on to say that this works particularly well if the site had been modelled on Flint Castle. The near-circular mound at the north-west corner would correspond to the Great Tower which stands at the south-east corner of that castle.

Was Richard the Engineer so proud of his work at Flint that he mirrored its plan in his own country house at Belgrave?

Alpraham (Highwayside)

Moat near Southley Farm   **NGR SJ 581593**

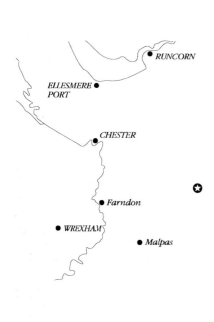

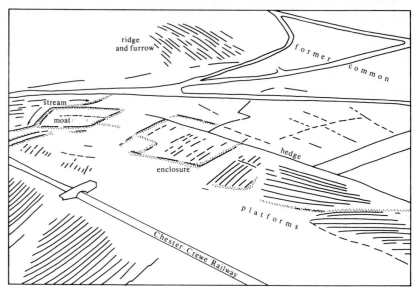

Ills 66-7 Alpraham moat,
looking NW

The precise nature of this former moat was first recognised from the air in July 1978 when the two photographs were taken. However, as is often the case, the spot was already known to historians locally as the site of a place called Southley.

The former moat is located immediately south of that part of Alpraham known as Highwayside, so named because the cottages which comprise the small community line the Tarporley to Nantwich road (the A51(T)). The date of this road, judged by the bulk of the cottages, cannot be later than the eighteenth/nineteenth centuries. Burdett's map of Cheshire, dated 1777, shows little development at Highwayside and none at all at Southley.

This much older site of Southley consists of two green lanes which come from the present A51(T) and converge near the point where the former moat may be seen. The triangular area of land between these green lanes is now bisected by the road leading to Bunbury. A search by local historians amongst the records of the Mostyn Estate has shown that this triangular area of land was once known as Southley Common, the name also noted on Bryant's map of the

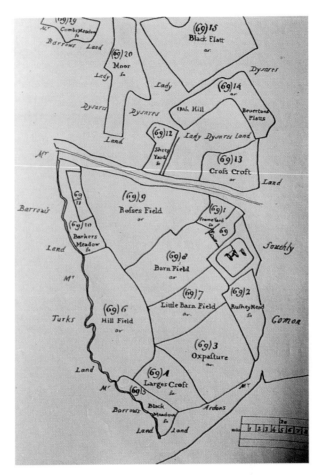

County Palatine of Cheshire dated 1831. (It should perhaps be mentioned here that the Mostyn family's interest in Alpraham derives from their descent from the Beeston family of Beeston).

The name Southley Common and the proximity of a Southley Farm suggest that the moated site must have been that of a formerly existing Southley manor house. According to Dodgson a 'Maner' de Southlegh' was mentioned in 1305. He also writes that a hall of Southley was mentioned in 1494.

The former moat stands just south of the point where the green lanes join the road to Bunbury. It is not immediately recognisable at ground level as a moat, although the platform it encloses is quite prominent. It measures some 68 m by 37 m and is aligned approximately north-east to south-west.

The moat ditch has long been filled in along much of the short north-east side, and the long south-east side has been altered. It is most obvious along the other two sides. The ditch has been captured by a small stream or it may be that the stream always fed the moat. The stream joins the moat at its south-west corner where there may have been a sluice gate arrangement or some fish-ponds. The complete outline of the moat can now only be seen and readily interpreted from the air, with a low sun emphasising any remaining original hollows.

The identification of this moated manor house site was made difficult by the existence of an adjoining 'moated' feature (centre of Ill 66) which is partly cut across, at a slight angle, by a hedge of later date. This second feature proved to be a rectangular enclosure with a narrow ditch on two sides and a drop in level onto what is now marshy ground on the other two sides. There is what appears

Ill 68 (l) Alpraham green lane leading off the A51(T), looking SE
Ill 69 (r) 18th-century estate map, showing Southley Common (Mostyn Papers)

References
Bryant 1831
Burdett 1777, vi
Dodgson 1971, 300-1
Ormerod 1882, **2**, 279-81

to be a house platform in one corner. It was thought at first that this second enclosure was part of the same manor house complex that was formed by the green lanes and the first moat. However, it is not so regarded now and is thought to be later in date.

While the secondary ditched enclosure must be more recent than the old manor house moat, it cannot be very recent because of the hedge which cuts across it. In addition, the sun was very low in the sky when the photograph was taken and has revealed extremely slight traces of ploughing within the enclosure. In view of this evidence, it is thought that this second enclosure probably dates from the late eighteenth or early nineteenth centuries, and had nothing to do with the old manor of Southley. A post-1732 estate map (Ill 69) accompanying the Mostyn Papers (University of Wales, Mostyn Papers No 8700) shows only one moat, which encloses a building. This is presumed to be the old moated site and not the adjoining ditched enclosure. Southley Common is named on the map but the moated site is not.

It is not known whether or not there was a small community at Southley, as well as the manor house. The existence of a common suggests that there may have been one. No traces of any tofts or other dwelling sites can now be recognised. Three or four low platforms can be seen between the bottom right-hand corner of the photograph and the ditched enclosure in the centre. These are probably geological in origin. On the other hand, they do have ridge and furrow on them - a straight ridge and furrow which is in alignment with the length of each individual platform. This almost suggests that they were, at one time, small, individually cultivated plots.

The ridge and furrow ploughing in the fields to the south of the site is interrupted by the nineteenth-century Chester to Crewe railway line or, in some fields, merely comes up to it. In both cases, the ploughing is post-medieval in character inasmuch as it is straight, comparatively narrow and covers almost everything except the old moat and the common. The ridge and furrow to the west of the site is also straight and comparatively narrow. It stops on a prominent curving bank which broadly follows the curve of the western green lane (Ill 68). This bank is probably no more than an unusually well defined headland. No ploughing consistent with the fourteenth- and fifteenth-century occupation of the site, as cited by Dodgson, can be identified in the immediate vicinity.

According to Ormerod, writing about Alpraham township, 'a farmhouse called the Moat-house from a large moat with which it is surrounded' probably occupied 'the site of the old mansion of the Alprahams'. This means that there were apparently two moated sites not only within the parish of Bunbury but within the township of Alpraham. This creates an anomaly because Cheshire moats, with two exceptions, seem to be on the basis of one per township.

THE ploughing of the land into a series of crests or ridges separated by shallow valleys or furrows has produced a common feature in the midland counties and in much of west Cheshire. The antiquary calls this feature 'ridge (or rig) and furrow'; the Cheshire farmer calls it 'butt and rein (or rean)', the butt being the ridge and the rein the furrow or valley between two ridges.

Whatever Cheshire farmers think about their butt and rein today (and there seems to be more than one theory about it), its original purpose was to rid the clay lands of as much standing water as possible. Needless to say, this was in the days long before ceramic agricultural drainpipes were introduced.

The oldest varieties of ridge and furrow, which pass beneath the hedgerows and clearly belong to an older open field system of farming, invariably run downhill towards riverside meadows, or run towards a ditch or stream, or they link up with other areas of ridge and furrow which do this.

This attempt at land drainage was by no means always successful, as can readily be seen during the winter months, for example along the River Dee between Eccleston and Chester. The place-name Wetreins Green, in the Dee valley, is interesting in this respect. The ridge and furrow ploughing could not have worked particularly well, and the reins or furrows apparently remained wet.

To ridge up a flat field in this way from virgin ground could not have been easy and depended as much on the skill of the ploughman as on the quality of his plough and strength and manoeuvrability of his draught animals. The process of doing this is equally difficult to explain in simple terms. W G Hoskins (1979, 48) puts it simply as 'the up-and-down ploughing of the long narrow strips, with a certain type of plough, threw the soil towards the centre of the strip, so producing a high ridge'. His description is correct but assumes that the width of the strip was formed in this way into one ridge. That was not the case, at least in Cheshire. A strip, which was the unit of land holding, could have two, three or more ridges, which were the units of ploughing, within its width. Essentially the same process applied for building up ridges in Cheshire as elsewhere, but the passage of the plough up and down the length of the strip was a little more complicated than Hoskins implied with his 'one strip - one ridge' description.

A large team of oxen was used to draw the plough in the Middle Ages and this would need considerable space in which to turn at the end of a strip in order to come back again, even if it did so along a different strip. The plough team, therefore, had to approach the headlands at the ends of each plough strip at an angle rather than head-on. This is believed to be the reason for the curving of much of the ridge and furrow into a reversed letter-S shape. This feature, known to landscape historians as an aratral (or ploughing) curve, is held to be diagnostic of ploughing dating from the medieval period. Ill 70 shows an area of typical medieval ridge and furrow at Hatton.

Not all ridge and furrow dates from the Middle Ages by any means. At that time, fields were unhedged open tracts of land divided into strip holdings by nothing more than banks of unploughed turf or double furrows or lines of stones. In contrast, ridge and furrow which is narrow and straight and which has been ploughed between hedgerows clearly belongs to later times when Cheshire had largely been divided into the pattern of enclosed fields which we see today (Ills 78-9). It can also be said that the progression from wide curving, and even meandering, ridges to narrower straighter ones, probably illustrates the gradual

7

THE MEDIEVAL PERIOD

AGRICULTURE

replacement of the ox by the horse as a draught animal. Illustrations 78-9 show quite a good example of this kind of ploughing contrasting with and obliterating medieval ridge and furrow.

Cheshire farmers will tell you that their fathers used to plough in this way, although they seem uncertain why they did so. There can be little doubt that the straight, regular and narrow ridge and furrow ploughed between hedgerows, represents this recent practice. It was probably finally brought to an end by new, quicker farming practices and technology engendered by the First World War.

There is a third variety of ridge and furrow which seems to lie between the two described above, both in type and in date. This, like the curving medieval variety, passes beneath the hedgerows and plainly belongs to fields which were still open tracts of land. Unlike the medieval variety, however, it does not have a deliberately reversed-S curve. Indeed, it is not curved at all in that sense. The ridges are usually long and narrow, are generally of equal width and are parallel to each other. The whole body of this ridge and furrow will often bend to follow the curve of a river or other feature. The ridges also have the peculiarity of tending to expand or fan out as they come up towards a headland. It can be demonstrated at some sites that this ridge and furrow is post-medieval in date, if only because it passes over medieval features such as abandoned moated sites. Illustration 76 shows a good example of it near Woodhey Chapel at Faddiley. The evidence so far available suggests that this variety of ridge and furrow is indeed post-medieval but not recent. It would seem that the best context for it is from the late seventeenth century to sometime in the eighteenth century.

As has been written elsewhere, the three varieties of ridge and furrow which have been described above should not be seen as distinct immutable types, each with an absolute date range. They should rather be seen as salient points in a progression from early to late forms. They illustrate a gradual replacement of open by enclosed fields and the gradual, and perhaps not so gradual, introduction of new farming technology. One must remember the innovations of the Industrial Revolution and in particular of Jethro Tull (1676-1741), who revolutionised agriculture in England.

As the years progressed, the original purpose of ridge and furrow as a means of drainage seemed to be forgotten. There are many examples to be found in west Cheshire where the old curving ridge and furrows, draining onto riverside meadow or into a brook, has been overlain and been largely obliterated by a straighter variety laid down in a completely different direction.

Hatton

Ridge and furrow ploughing north-east of Hatton Hall   **NGR SJ 476616** (centre of photograph)

III 70 Ridge and furrow ploughing at Hatton, looking NE

The aerial photograph, taken from the south-west in August 1976, shows a very fine area of wide, curved, medieval-style ridge and furrow consisting of a series of reversed-S curves which give it a meandering appearance. Each ridge finishes at a headland, at least one of which may at one time have served as a convenient farm track or field way.

The ridge and furrow has been cut into by later marl pits, three of which may be seen towards the top centre of the photograph. A hedge running upwards from the bottom left corner of the photograph is also later than the ridge and furrow. In addition, the photograph shows the line of the old Chester to Whitchurch railway diverging from the main Chester to Crewe and London (Euston) line. Both these railways cut through the ridge and furrow, which can still be clearly seen from a train.

Three other features of interest, especially to the agricultural historian, may be seen in the photograph. One is the curious dying away of some ridges between others, for example, at the bottom right-hand corner. This cannot be explained easily and, according to some landscape historians, is peculiar to Cheshire. This peculiarity, and the occasional 'lurch' of a group of ridges to one side, hardly gives the impression of neatly ploughed, corn-growing individual strip holdings as found in many of the midland counties. On the contrary, the impression is of open pasture land which has been ridge and furrow ploughed for drainage. While this may be generally acceptable to historians for Tudor and later times, it has not, so far as the writer is aware, been seriously considered for the medieval period.

The second feature of interest is the subdivision of some of the wide medieval ridges at a later date (centre right of the photograph, against the Chester to Crewe railway). The third is the introduction of additional, narrow ridges between the old, wide ones (centre of the photograph).

Writing in 1845, the agricultural historian W Palin implied that the extra ridges had been ploughed to facilitate land drainage still further in order to improve the pasture for cattle. Palin did not know when this had been done but wrote that it was at some time in the past, ie, well before 1845 but after the Middle Ages when the original wide curving ridge and furrow was formed.

Palin's observations relate specifically to the post-medieval period, but they accord well with what has been said above regarding the possibility of there having been extensive pasture land in Cheshire during the medieval period.

References

Palin 1845, 23

Eyton

Remnants of hedged strip fields at Gyfelia **NGR SJ 326452** (centre of photograph)

Ills 71-2 Remnants of strip fields, looking E

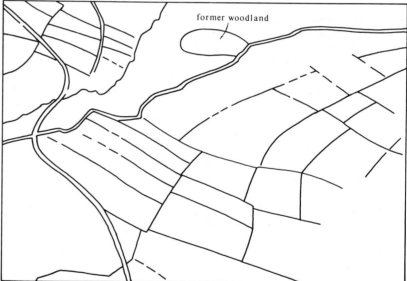

At the end of the Middle Ages, farming practices changed in most of England. Open lands, which had largely been devoted to growing corn, were increasingly enclosed and converted to pasture for sheep or cattle. Indeed, too much land was converted and in the reign of Elizabeth a good proportion had by law to be put back to growing crops.

The process of conversion to pasture perhaps began rather earlier in Cheshire than elsewhere, but the effects on the landscape were the same. Hedges and ditches were in many cases put in regardless of the extent and direction of ridge and furrow; or conveniently small and rectangular parcels of ridge and furrow were enclosed as individual fields. Alternatively, portions of the old strip holdings were hedged about to make long narrow fields. Such hedged fields often appear on nineteenth-century tithe award maps where they have long disappeared on the ground. The map for Lower Bunbury (Ill 73) is a good example.

The aerial photograph, taken in August 1988 looking east, shows a landscape of fields which essentially consist of portions of old strips. Those in the lower left-hand quarter of the photograph show that the strips ran from east to

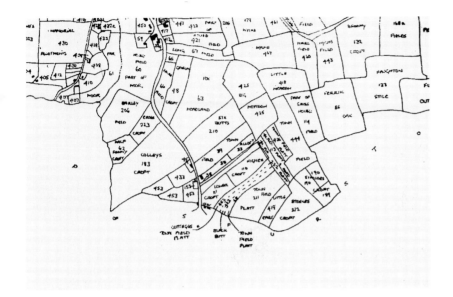

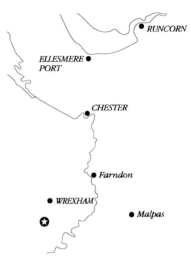

Ill 73 Lower Bunbury tithe map (Cheshire R O EDT 76/2)

west. They met and stopped against other strips, also fossilised in the hedged fields, curving down from the top right-hand corner towards the bottom of the picture. These narrow fields have even retained some of the curvature of the old ridge and furrow ploughing of the strips, which clearly marks them as medieval. The sub-circular field at the top centre of the photograph was probably a small wood or coppice which was cut down and the tree stumps removed to add to the cultivated land.

Strip cultivation, such as that fossilised in the landscape near Eyton, is usually regarded as a medieval English phenomenon rather than a Welsh one. It was not unknown in lowland Wales, however, even away from such English influences as Edward I's castles and boroughs. It was possibly introduced during the Roman period. Nevertheless, traces of ridge and furrow ploughing and of hedged former strips are not generally common beyond Offa's Dyke.

Hedged strips are quite numerous in the Wrexham area, especially in the vicinity of Worthenbury. This is historically interesting as this area is well east of Offa's Dyke. The strip fields photographed near Eyton are, on the other hand, only 1 km east of Offa's Dyke and some 0.75 km from the earlier Wat's Dyke. That is to say, they are a long way west of the present national boundary. They may surely be regarded as the successors to early strip fields which would themselves have represented the expansion of the English kingdom of Mercia beyond the River Dee and the intensive cultivation of formerly Welsh land right up to the then newly constructed dykes. The name Eyton, for example, is purely English, although the place is now once more in Wales.

Mollington

Ridge and furrow ploughing east of Mollington Grange NGR SJ 390694 (centre of photograph)

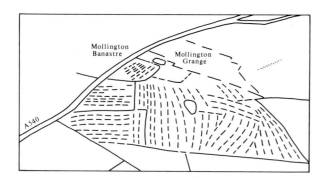

Ills 74-5 Ridge and furrow plough-ing east of Mollington Grange, looking NW

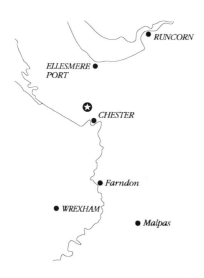

The aerial photograph was taken from the south-east in February 1983. The area of ridge and furrow shown adjacent to Mollington Grange is very near to the Mollington Banastre Hotel, which can be seen opposite Mollington Grange in the photograph.

Mollington Banastre is the old name for Little Mollington, which is now included with Great Mollington in modern Mollington, within the parish of Backford. The suffix 'Banastre', which is recorded in 1286, derived from a Lancashire man named Robert de Banastre (or Bannister) to whom the manor was granted by Edward I. It is also interesting to note that the area of ridge and furrow, as well as the modern hotel, is adjacent to the moated site of Little Mollington Hall.

The ridge and furrow is, for the most part, wide and curving and of medieval character. Some of the ridges die out between others. They are also cut into by waterlogged marl pits (there is one in the very centre of the photograph). A series of narrow ditches near the Chester to Birkenhead road (A540) (to the left of centre of the photograph) are made prominent by the low February sun. These mark the outlines of small fields whose hedges have been taken up. While it was normal for small convenient parcels of ridge and furrow to be hedged about in this way in post-medieval times, the hedging was not always confined to them. In the photograph, the lower of the three small former fields bordering the road seems to have taken in two or three ridges from an adjoining patch of ridge and furrow.

The area of medieval ridge and furrow in the centre of the photograph would at one time have been part of an open, unhedged field system which presuma-bly belonged to the manor of Little Mollington, and therefore to Little Mollington Hall. The existence of a farmhouse named Mollington Grange seems to be no more than a coincidence; there does not seem to have been an ecclesiastical grange, or monastic farm, here that belonged to one of the great religious hous-es of the area, for example, St Werburgh's Abbey or Birkenhead Priory. Little Mollington was at one time included in the parish of St Mary-on-the Hill, Ches-ter, and there may have been a connection between the two. However, this is unlikely, and the name 'Grange' is probably post-medieval, possibly compara-tively recent; the term 'grange' does not seem to be linked to any of the old field-names in the area.

AT the end of the Middle Ages, great estates were built up, especially from the time of Elizabeth I onwards. The castle and the defended manor house were gradually replaced by the stately home set within its ornamental park. But life for the peasant farmer in the Cheshire countryside altered little between the medieval period and the eighteenth century.

The eighteenth and nineteenth centuries are usually regarded as the great periods of land enclosure which brought great changes to the peasant farmers' way of life. This picture is not entirely true for Cheshire, however, nor for many western counties of England. According to the traveller John Leland, writing in the sixteenth century, much of the land in these areas had already been enclosed into the hedged fields that we see today. This had been done privately by agreement between the various landowners, and between them and their tenant farmers.

Nevertheless, the eighteenth century did bring the great changes to the countryside. Hard-wearing macadamised roads were developed, canals were constructed and the steam engine was invented. All three affected transport and agricultural practice.

Jethro Tull, a lawyer who interested himself in farming methods, was probably the greatest instigator of change. He found the traditional medieval methods quite unacceptable and representing no more than subsistence farming. He revolutionised farming with his mechanical inventions and by the sound advice which followed his shrewd observations of traditional methods. As a result, fields became larger again to accommodate the machinery which has culminated in the fast-moving tractor and the combine harvester of today.

By the 1770s, a few men of vision had begun to question the condition of rural cottages and those who occupied them. Pattern books began to be published with suggested simple designs for cottages of brick with serviceable slate or tile replacing the traditional thatch. Model farms were designed, villages were replanned and much improved accommodation was provided for farm workers who, in many cases, had been little more than house beggars. In the nineteenth century the concern felt by men like Robert Owen, Lord Shaftesbury and Dr Barnardo for the poor and under-privileged in the industrial towns and cities was reflected in the Cheshire countryside by landlords such as the Marquis of Westminster and Lord Tollemache. The villages of Eccleston, Aldford and Churton are notable examples near Chester of their improvements.

The eighteenth and nineteenth centuries and the Industrial Revolution have brought many benefits to Cheshire and other counties. Unfortunately, they have also brought with them the means of destroying our landscape at an unimaginable speed.

8

POST-MEDIEVAL AGRICULTURE

Faddiley

Ridge and furrow ploughing near to Woodhey Chapel   **NGR SJ 573527**

Ills 76-7 Ridge and furrow ploughing near Woodhey Chapel, looking S

This photograph, taken looking south in July 1982, shows several interesting features. On the left there is a walled enclosure with a small isolated building on its right-hand side. This is Woodhey Chapel, a private chapel belonging to Woodhey Hall, a mansion of the Wilbraham family, which formerly stood a little way to the east. The chapel, which is a fine example of late seventeenth- or early eighteenth-century architecture, was linked to the hall by a raised causeway. This can be seen to the right of the chapel in the photograph.

The enclosed square, now a paddock, was once a walled garden associated with the hall. According to documentary evidence held in the Cheshire County Record Office, Woodhey Hall, which was a building of seventeenth-century character but possibly of earlier origin, stood near the right-hand corner of the walled garden and was parallel to its long sides and to the chapel. This has proved valuable in dating the ridge and furrow ploughing in the adjoining fields.

The ploughing, which covers the lower half of the photograph, is wide and passes under the hedgerows of adjoining fields. It does not, however, have the reversed-S and apparent meander which would have dated it to the medieval period. Nor does this type of ridge and furrow stop short of medieval monuments, such as abandoned moats, but often carries on over them. Unlike those of the medieval period in Cheshire, these ridges are usually regular in width and spacing and suggest ploughing by something other than large teams of oxen: probably a very much smaller team of horses which was more manageable.

This ridge and furrow has two other interesting characteristics, namely that the whole group of ridges tends to turn together, in parallel, along the bend of a river or other feature. They also have a tendency to spread outwards as they approach a headland at the end of their run. Both these peculiarities can be seen

76

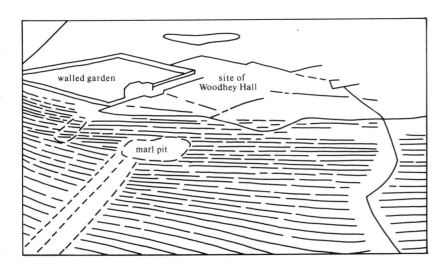

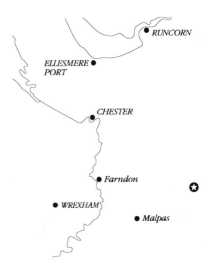

in the photograph. At the left of the photograph may also be seen a double headland interrupted by an old filled-in marl pit.

In the very centre of the photograph, a slightly ditched corner of a rectangular feature can be seen. This makes a re-entrant angle in the largely grubbed-up hedge which runs across the picture. In doing this, the feature has cut into and obliterated some of the ridge and furrow. The latter, therefore, is plainly older than it. The rectangular feature is, in turn, parallel with the walled garden and chapel and with the former lines of the demolished Woodhey Hall. It can therefore be reasonably accepted as dating from the same period and was probably a garden terrace or something similar.

Woodhey Hall, as shown on the drawings held by the County Record Office, was a seventeenth-century building. It was demolished during the eighteenth century. The 'garden terrace' feature, therefore, is likely to date from the seventeenth or eighteenth century and the ridge and furrow, into which it cuts, must be older than it, but not medieval. The date range which suggests itself for this type of ridge and furrow is from the sixteenth or seventeenth to perhaps the late eighteenth centuries.

Shocklach Oviatt

Recent ridge and furrow ploughing   **NGR SJ 443487** (Centre of photograph)

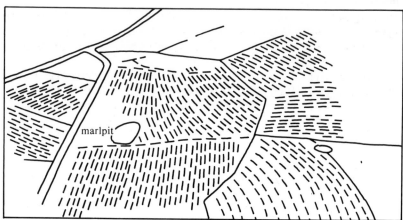

marlpit

Ills 78-9 Ridge and furrow ploughing at Shocklach Oviatt, looking NW

The photograph, looking north-west, was taken on 3 January 1979 after a fall of snow. Snow cover and poor light conditions, while adequate for flying a light aircraft, can make the identification of small places served by minor roads rather difficult and the precise location of features almost impossible. Success depends largely upon detailed map study of the general area photographed as soon as possible after the flight.

This photograph shows very clearly two periods of ridge and furrow ploughing. The greater part of the land is covered with wide curving ridges, typical of those produced by ox-drawn ploughs in the Middle Ages. For the most part, these can be seen to be running underneath hedgerows and quite clearly belong to open unhedged fields. The greater age of this ploughing is also emphasised by the existence of at least one marl pit which has been cut through the old ridges.

The bottom left-hand part of the photograph shows a very different type of ridge and furrow. This is straight, regular in width, and has been ploughed between the hedges, ie it dates from a time when the open fields had been enclosed. Part of the hedge running horizontally across the picture at this point has been destroyed, but its line can still be clearly seen just clipping an old marl pit. It is quite obvious from the photograph that the narrow ridge and furrow, ploughed between these hedgerows, interrupts the flowing curves of the ☞

Hatton

Ridge and furrow ploughing adjacent to Hatton Hall   **NGR SJ 468612** (centre of photograph)

III 80 Ridge and furrow ploughing near Hatton Hall, looking NE

This almost vertical photograph was taken in September 1984. It shows curving ridge and furrow ploughing of medieval character. No doubt it originally formed part of an open field system, as it can be very faintly made out continuing across some of the adjoining fields.

The ridge and furrow has, however, been altered at a later date, possibly after the hedges had been planted, by having an additional narrow ridge created in the furrow (rean) between two ridges (butts). This has already been referred to above. The practice was mentioned by W Palin in 1845. He wrote of Cheshire dairy farms that 'A large portion of the flat clay-land has been formed, ages ago, into butts or loons (ie, the ridges) varying in width from 15 feet to 50 feet or more. Where this is the case, the form is scarcely ever altered, unless by a few furrows being ridged up in the rein (ie the furrow) to the width of 5 or 6 feet'. This was evidently done to achieve the best possible drainage of the heavy soil, this being of paramount importance for good pasture with a view to getting a good milk yield, and doubtless the best quality Cheshire cheese.

References
Palin 1845, 8

☞older variety and is very much younger. Its straightness, the constant width of the ridges and their short lengths within an enclosed field, suggest that the plough was horse-drawn.

This second, straight variety of ridge and furrow always seems to be the most recent in any stratification of the farmed landscape, and portions of older, curving varieties can often still be seen showing through it when it is viewed from the air. It was probably the variety of ridge and furrow still being ploughed by Cheshire farmers at the beginning of the twentieth century. It is also interesting to note that it does not always follow the slopes of the ground as the older varieties did. In fact, it can sometimes be seen to be at right-angles to an earlier variety on the same spot. It is probable that, with the advent of clay agricultural drainage pipes, its original purpose of draining the land was largely forgotten. By the turn of the century, if not before, it is possible that land was being ploughed in this way more out of habit than anything else.

Coddington

Steam ploughing south-east of Edgerley Farm   **NGR SJ 438567**

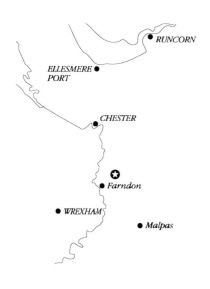

III 81 Steam ploughing south-east of Edgerley Farm

The second half of the nineteenth century was perhaps memorable for the efforts made by enlightened and determined individuals to improve the living and social conditions of the urban working classes. It was no less so in the countryside, although this has not been so well publicised. The owners of some, if not all, great estates did what they perceived to be their duty to improve the lot of their farm workers and their estate dwellers in general. Farmhouses were rebuilt, new up-to-date cottages provided, whole villages replanned and landscapes transformed. The Grosvenor family of Eaton Hall near Chester were among these improving landlords.

Not only were properties improved in this way, but the latest in farming technologies were adopted wherever possible. Amongst these was steam ploughing, which was fairly exceptional and likely to be found only on the lands of these improving landlords.

The photograph, taken in July 1976, shows a good example of land ploughed in this way. To describe it simply, the technique usually involved positioning a steam traction engine at one end of the field to be ploughed, and a pulley arrangement, or possibly a second traction engine, at the other end. By this means, a multiple plough was pulled along the field to the far end, turning the soil as it went. The plough was then re-angled, or repositioned as necessary, and pulled back again, turning over a new length of soil. A long block of ground was ploughed in this way and the whole contraption then moved to plough the next block. This process produced what can only be termed 'ridge and furrow' as shown in the photograph. The ridges are, however, very straight, very regular and very mechanical in appearance. The photograph also shows much older, probably medieval, ridge and furrow in the fields on either side of the steam-ploughed block. The steam ploughing has cut through the older ridge and furrow, obliterating it and making it appear discontinuous.

A 'house platform' may be seen at the bottom right-hand corner of the photograph. A pair of cottages formerly stood here, fronting onto the road. When buildings are demolished they frequently leave platforms such as this owing to incomplete clearance of the debris. However, sometimes platforms were deliberately created to raise the dwelling clear of damp ground. Often they can also be the result of activities such as the constant digging of garden soil, laying of successive paths and the general build-up of small occupation debris.

MOST of the farmland of Cheshire had been divided into enclosed fields well before the eighteenth century, largely for holding livestock, especially cattle. This process of enclosure continued in the eighteenth and nineteenth centuries, when large dairy farms were developed. These made up great estates centred upon country mansions set within ornamental parkland.

The farm buildings were in most cases designed by local builders, but there were exceptions to this: for example, John Douglas of Chester designed many of the excellent farm complexes on the Duke of Westminster's Eaton estate. The designers of the great country mansions are better known, having been, in most cases, national figures within the architectural world. For example, while Cholmondeley Castle had additions by Sir John Smirke, and Alfred Waterhouse (designer of Manchester Town Hall) was responsible for the Gothic-style Eaton Hall. The latter was demolished in 1972 and was replaced with a modern house.

Eaton Hall, Cholmondeley Castle and several others were replacements for earlier houses, often on the same sites. Others in the county, however, are still the original medieval or Tudor structures which have been improved and enlarged to meet the needs and changing lifestyles of later generations. Little Moreton Hall (also known as Moreton Old Hall) is a good example of this, where the spectacular black and white entrance block is the result of an Elizabethan long gallery being built, rather precariously, over an earlier gatehouse.

The parkland which surrounds the great houses was not a carefully nurtured and managed natural development. Far from it: most ornamental parks were deliberately set out and planted either under the direction of the estate's owner or by a person who possessed a special skill in such work. One of the best known of these landscape architects, as they came to be called, was Humphrey Repton. He designed Tatton Park for Lord Egerton, while Joseph Paxton, designer of the Crystal Palace, laid out the nine terraces immediately behind Tatton Hall. Eaton Park near Chester affords another good example of design by well known people. The fine gardens around Eaton Hall were the work of Sir Edwin Lutyens and Elizabeth Jekyll. Other great Cheshire houses also have well thought out schemes of landscaping and planting. Among these are Bolesworth Castle, Cholmondeley Castle and Arley Hall.

Cheshire villages, all of which in the west of the county date from at least the medieval period, were managed as part of the great estates. This was especially true where the landlord had the welfare of his tenants at heart. Such landowners frequently set about a rebuilding programme where cottages were dilapidated and outmoded in their design. As was the case with the mansions, well known architects were often employed for the work of re-planning and reconstruction. In the case of the Eaton estate, for example, John Douglas designed most of the houses in the model villages of Eccleston, Saighton and Pulford, while Dodleston was not only given new buildings but the village road layout was considerably altered as well.

THE GREAT ESTATES

Cholmondeley

Cholmondeley Castle and Park **NGR SJ 536514**

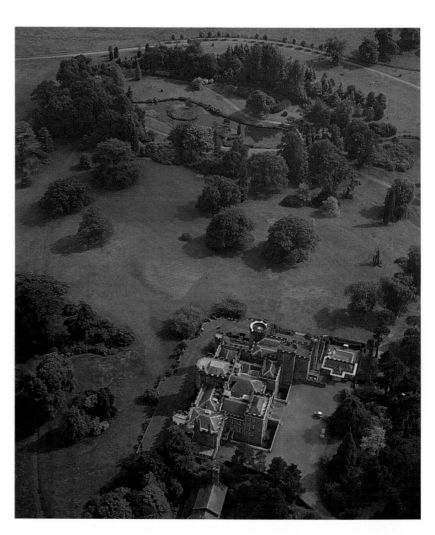

III 82 Chomondeley Castle and Park, looking S

References
North-West Civic Trust 1983, 135-7

This aerial view taken in June 1983 looks south and shows the castle almost in plan, but only a small part of the extensive and beautiful parkland. Near the top of the picture there is a small elongated lake with trees in full leaf and bushes, probably rhododendrons, in full flower. It does not show the two large lakes to the north-east and south-east of the castle, namely Chapel Mere and Deer Park Mere.

The Cholmondeley family have lived here since the twelfth century, but the present castle is a nineteenth-century creation in the Gothic Revival style. The original house stood within the park and was replaced by one designed by Sir John Vanburgh, who also designed Blenheim Palace (Oxfordshire) and Castle Howard (Yorkshire). The present castle, which is on higher ground than its forerunners, was completed for the first Marquess of Cholmondeley in 1804 and was built to his own design. Further towers and battlements were added later to the designs of Sir Robert Smirke, designer of the British Museum.

There is also a detached family chapel which is known to have been heavily restored in the seventeenth century. The date of its foundation is unknown, but it is thought that it may have been built as early as 1200. There are references to the chapel of Cholmondeley in 1285.

The gardens at Cholmondeley Castle were also created in the early nineteenth century and are renowned for their roses and banks of flowering herbaceous plants with their tumbling streams and lakes.

Peckforton

Victorian castle   **NGR SJ 533580**

III 83 Peckforton Castle, looking N

Peckforton Castle was designed by Anthony Salvin about 1845 as a country house for the first Lord Tollemache, who owned extensive estates in the area. It is dramatically perched amid parkland at a gap in Cheshire's Central Ridge and looks across - almost in opposition - to the ancient castle at Beeston. Peckforton Castle was intended to be fully visible but now it is almost hidden by woodland except for its towers.

Peckforton is a fine piece of Victorian architecture and has an imposing main entrance gateway on the road below the ridge. From here, a long track climbs upwards to a tall, comparatively narrow gateway complete with a portcullis. This gateway leads to an extensive bailey or courtyard, with the tall buildings of the castle along its far side, while lower buildings such as the chapel and workshops and so on occupy the other sides. The main buildings have a high tower, a great hall, a crypt and other pseudo-medieval apartments. The architectural details are closely modelled on those of Caernarfon castle, the distinctive 'flat' Caernarfon arch being much in evidence.

Lord Tollemache was the sole member of his family to live here, but it has attracted several other tenants through the years. It has also been the location for several films and television programmes requiring a medieval setting.

The photograph was taken looking north in October 1978 with the low autumn sun reflecting the warm glow of the red sandstone of which the castle is built.

References
Bott & Williams 1975, 44
North-West Civic Trust 1983, 171

Knutsford

Tatton Hall and Park   **NGR SJ 745816**

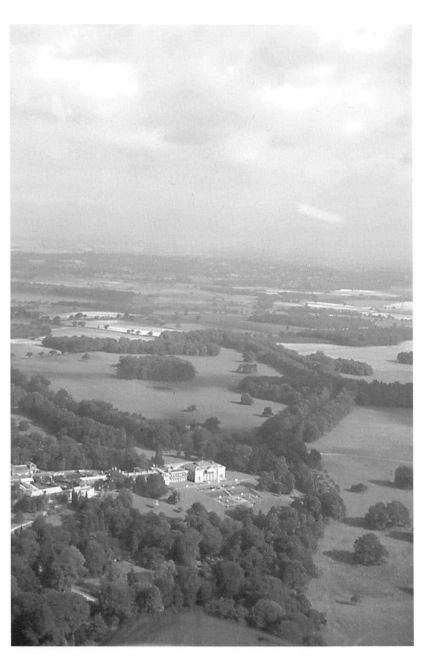

Ill 84 Tatton Hall and Park,
looking E

References
North-West Civic Trust 1983
Williams 1984

Illustration 84, taken in September 1976, looks east towards Rostherne Mere and shows Tatton Hall in the centre foreground with two fine avenues of mature trees leading away from it. The present hall, completed in 1813 to designs by Samuel and Lewis Wyatt, replaced an eighteenth-century house on the same site. This earlier house was built for John Egerton, the first member of his family to live at Tatton.

Tatton Hall stands within the great park which was designed by Humphrey Repton, the well known landscape architect. He created the park, in the accepted manner of his day, by clearing away roads, buildings and anything else he thought to be inappropriate, and replaced them with natural-looking hillocks, lakes and clumps of trees. It is said that he recommended the removal of the tree-lined avenues seen in the aerial photograph. These were already in existence and were the pride and joy of the then Lord Egerton, who fortunately resisted Repton's arguments.

Humphrey Repton recommended the formation of a lake where Melchett Mere is now found. Lord Egerton, however, felt he could not afford the additional expense and rejected the idea. However, brine pumping in the not-too-distant salt areas around Northwich led to subsidence in Tatton Park and the present lake appeared almost overnight. It was named after Lord Melchett, who at that time was chairman of the Brine Pumping Board.

The terraces seen in the photograph between the hall and the belt of trees at the bottom of the picture were laid out by Sir Joseph Paxton, who designed the Crystal Palace for the Great Exhibition of 1851. He also designed Birkenhead Park, which became the model for Central Park in New York.

Repton's magnificent creation is eight miles in circumference and consists of about a thousand acres of hills, grassland and trees. Lord Egerton apparently wished to screen the park from the town of Knutsford, and a thick belt of trees was deliberately planted at the south-western corner of the park for that purpose.

The present Tatton Hall and its forerunners on the same site were not the first halls within Tatton Park. There is an older building, which belonged to a succession of families before the Egertons. This is known as Tatton Old Hall and stands 1 km (about ½ mile) to the east. This is a brick structure, which careful examination and archaeological excavation have revealed originally to have been a timber-framed building. One wing is the remaining half of a great hall built in the late fifteenth to early sixteenth century. The other wing, also of timber, was added in the Elizabethan period. The hall was rebuilt piecemeal in brickwork, without disturbing the heavy roof, in the seventeenth and eighteenth centuries.

Tatton Old Hall stood just outside the village of Tatton, which is Cheshire's only deserted village of any size. It was already in decline when Repton swept the last remaining buildings away in the early nineteenth century. The village had a very long history, and occupation on that spot has been traced from prehistoric times, through the Middle Ages, to the early nineteenth century. Archaeologically speaking, this continuity probably makes it the key site for understanding the pattern of settlement in Cheshire and in the north-west generally. Illustration 84 only shows a small part of this extensive park.

10

MISCELLANEOUS FEATURES

THERE are many features in the Cheshire landscape which are either un-common or do not fit conveniently into the chapter headings in this book. They may be banks, channels, depressions or curiously shaped enclosures, most of which were apparently man-made but whose origins have been forgotten and whose purpose is now difficult to explain. A bank may have been defensive; on the other hand, it may simply be an old ploughing headland. A dry channel may be an abandoned canal branch, but it could have been a hollow way or sunken road. A series of low mounds may have been a Bronze Age cemetery, but they could be natural in origin. A small banked enclosure was probably just an animal pound, but it may have been a Civil War gun emplacement. There are many features that remain to be explained, such as potential mill pools, quarries and mining pits, medieval cultivation plots, and military works perhaps dating to the First or Second World Wars. Only by carefully considering such features in their wider context, in relation to other features, and ultimately by excavating them archaeologically, can they be interpreted correctly.

Four relatively uncommon sites or features have been selected for illustration in this book. They are old peat diggings, a duck decoy, a water mill and a small enclosed site.

Water mills were formerly common in Cheshire, but with the advent of large-scale commercial milling, baking and bread distribution most of them have disappeared. Often all that is left is the former mill pool, recognisable in the landscape as a dry depression, usually triangular in shape. Its identification can sometimes be supported by the name 'Mill Field' on an old map of the locality.

The digging of peat was once a commonplace activity in areas where peat mosses occurred. It was usually a well organised local activity, with long thin and tapering slices of the moss, known as 'moss rooms', being allocated to individuals in a similar manner to that of cultivation strips in an open arable field. However, some of the more recent diggings were less organised and people presumably simply entered the moss and dug out peat where they wished.

The use of duck decoy pools was an ancient way of trapping wildfowl. Plainly an adaptation of a natural pool surrounded by woodland, they probably originated in the Neolithic period or possibly even earlier. Duck decoys are rare in all counties, and Cheshire is fortunate in having an unusually good example at Hale.

Several small areas enclosed by low banks may be seen from the air in the Cheshire landscape but, as mentioned above, their purpose is extraordinarily difficult to define, especially if they do not conform to any shape or size associated with a known purpose such as a Roman military camp or an Iron Age homestead. One of these, at Hough Bridge near Malpas, has been selected for illustration. As stated, it may have been a mill site, but it be part of the lost Anglo-Saxon settlement of *Depenbech*, whose extent and character is not really known from ancient records.

Tarporley

Features west of St Helen's Church   **NGR SJ 551624**

Ill 85 Features W of St Helen's Church, Tarporley

This aerial photograph, taken in 1984 approximately along the line of the now-completed Tarporley by-pass, shows an irregular chequerboard pattern of small raised and sunken features, some of which are waterlogged. They cannot be matched by anything similar in the county nor, indeed, elsewhere in the northwest. Enquiries locally elicited the information that the area was peaty and that the owners of the Portal estate in Tarporley had shown some interest in exploiting it on a small scale.

The features are quite unlike any of the 'moss rooms' or long narrow strips associated elsewhere in Cheshire with traditional peat digging (for example, at Congleton Moss). These were organized and exploited under strict rural practice and regulation, as indeed all land was in the Middle Ages. However, no information about the Tarporley features is available at present. They have therefore been recorded as probable local and fairly recent small-scale peat diggings. However, it should be recorded that alterations to the nearby church of St Helen, in the eighteenth and nineteenth centuries produced a considerable amount of rubble and other unwanted material. This is believed to have been dumped as fill in some of the old peat diggings.

Hale (near Widnes)

Duck decoy   **NGR SJ 478827**

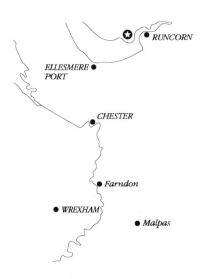

III 86 Hale duck decoy, looking NE

This is an unusually large duck decoy sited on the low-lying and marshy land south-east of the village of Hale.

Illustration 86 shows the essential requirements of a decoy. The first is an open stretch of water on which wildfowl can land. This is preferably screened by trees from the sight and sound of surrounding activities. The second requirement is that there should be one or more arms of water curving away from the lake or pool. Some examples have only one arm; others have two or three. This example has no less than five. Each arm or channel tapers away to nothing, as can be seen in the photograph, and is covered with netting which gets lower as the arm gets narrower. Each arm should have a fence along one side, with fairly frequent gaps in it.

The capture of wildfowl was effected by a man, usually accompanied by a dog, walking behind the fence and occasionally appearing at the gaps. Hopefully, he would entice one or more of the curious birds to swim down the length of the channel. The dog, meanwhile, was kept out of sight. When the birds had reached the narrow tip of the channel, the catcher suddenly appeared from behind the fence with his dog, making as much noise as possible. The birds took fright and flew upwards where, of course, they were caught in the netting.

Decoys have probably existed as long as man has been a wildfowler. The only clue to the age of the Hale decoy is a seventeenth-century dated stone on the side of a small dock where a boat may be tied up. It is likely that this is the date of this elaborate and symmetrical decoy, but it could have had a simpler forerunner.

This decoy is also unusual in having around it a narrow moat. When the author visited the site some years ago, this could only be crossed at one point by means of a swing bridge consisting only of one narrow plank of wood. This was usually kept locked and had to be unlocked and swung out, rather precariously, over the water.

The aerial photograph was taken from a height of about 1,000 feet in April 1982 and shows that some of the trees were dying. This was due partly to old age and partly to pollution of the fresh water by salt water seeping inland from the Mersey. These problems have since been rectified.

Status
Scheduled Ancient Monument

Stretton

Watermill and pool   **NGR SJ 454530**

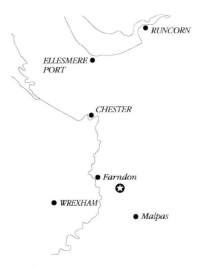

III 87 Watermill and pool, looking N

Stretton Mill, on the Carden Brook, is typical of the many mills which used to be found in Cheshire. Only a few remain: some are ruined and others have disappeared completely, leaving in one or two instances the former mill pool as a pleasing feature in the countryside. Stretton Mill is interesting in having two water wheels, one an overshot and the other an undershot wheel.

As may be seen in the photograph, taken in July 1977, the mill and all its appurtenances still exist. In fact, it was completely restored some years ago by Cheshire County Council and is in working order.

The triangular mill pool feeds the overshot wheel on the left (west) side of the mill almost directly, while a channel on the east side enters under the mill to turn the undershot wheel. The mill may be by-passed by letting the water flow along the spillway, seen running under the road from the top right-hand corner of the mill pool. The two tail races are not clearly visible in the photograph but pass under the road and combine into one channel which runs along the hedge immediately to the right of the former miller's cottage, seen above the mill. The latter has been enlarged in recent years and is now a two-storey house.

The mill is basically a timber-framed Elizabethan building with stone end walls to take the weight of the heavy wheels. Parts of the stonework inside and at the rear of the building have eighteenth-century dates, and the mill has plainly been renovated and added to in small ways over the years. Immediately to the west of the mill there is a small stable and store block which is now used as a display centre. This building, too, exhibits stonework of at least two periods.

Malpas

Features at Hough Bridge, possibly the site of a water mill   **NGR SJ 500461**

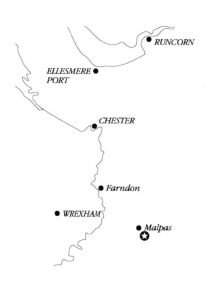

Ills 88-9 Features at Hough Bridge, looking SW

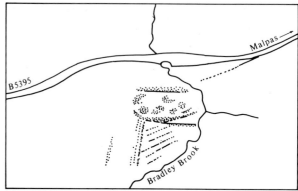

The aerial photograph, taken in December 1981 looking south-west, is of Hough Bridge on the Bradley Brook 1.75 km (just over 1 mile) from the cross at Malpas. The B5395 road is a little tortuous here and has had to be built up for the bridge crossing the narrow but deep little valley. This was probably the 'mal pas' or 'difficult passage' that gave Malpas its name and the Anglo-Saxon placename *Depenbech* or 'valley with a beck or little stream'.

The low sun has emphasised a low straight bank, running from left to right, in front of the bridge. A little below it is another bank which seems to be curved. The two banks enclose a D-shaped area on the left bank of the brook. The sun has also picked out what seem to be at least five low mounds within the enclosure. Traces of ridge and furrow ploughing can also be seen coming up to it.

A number of explanations suggest themselves for these features. The first is that the straight bank is the remnant of an embankment carrying an earlier road across the little valley. This is unlikely, as no trace of any road can be seen continuing the line of the bank. Another possibility is that the banks were part of a water mill complex on the Bradley Brook. This does not explain the low mounds, nor is there any trace of a mill pool. However, there was a Bradley Mill, presumably on the Bradley Brook, and Bradley itself, or at least the Hall Farm, is only 0.5 km (just under ¼ mile) from this site. It is also just possible that the features were connected with the small Anglo-Saxon settlement of *Depenbech* which seems to have migrated, in Norman times, to the castle at what was to become Malpas.

CHESTER is rightly presented to the public as a Roman foundation. However, the city is very much more than that. The buildings lining its main streets illustrate its history from Roman times to the present day. It was an important port and city in the Middle Ages, sufficiently so to have its own mint before the coming of the Normans, and it became - if only temporarily - a cathedral city (the seat of the Bishop of Lichfield) in 1075.

The principal roads of the Roman fortress are still clearly recognisable. Eastgate Street and Foregate Street are on the line of the *via principalis*; Bridge Street marks the *via praetoria* (which usually faced towards a potentially hostile area, presumably in this case the Welsh uplands), and Northgate Street lies over the *via decumana*. Chester's walls are substantially Roman on the north and east from St Martin's Gate (over the Inner Ring Road) to the New Gate. The Roman amphitheatre, or at least half of it, is prominent, and there is indeed substantial Roman extramural settlement on all but the northern side.

Features of the medieval city are naturally more prominent. These include the walls running south from the New Gate, along the Groves, past the Roodee and up to St Martin's Gate. These extensions to the Roman walls were first recorded in the twelfth century but may be earlier. Chester Castle, rebuilt as a neo-classical complex early in the nineteenth century, was founded by William the Conqueror in 1070.

The Old Dee Bridge, near to the Castle, is also medieval, being built in the fourteenth century, with frequent repairs since then. It is known to have replaced successive wooden bridges at the same point. The famous Mills of Dee, home of the jolly miller who worked and sang from morn 'til night, were at the northern end of this bridge.

There were at least nine churches inside the walled city, of which five survive, albeit given over to other purposes. These are Holy Trinity (now the Guildhall), St Peter's (an ecumenical centre), St Michael's (now the Heritage Centre), St Mary's (a conference and exhibition centre), and St Olave's. A sixth church, St Oswald's, is incorporated into the Cathedral. In addition to these, St John the Baptist, adjacent to the Roman amphitheatre, is still regularly used for Christian worship. It was allegedly founded in the seventh century. The first Norman bishop of Mercia moved his seat from Lichfield to the larger and much more important town of Chester. He set about remodelling and improving the old Saxon church of St John to give it the dignity appropriate to a cathedral church, but after his death his succesor removed the see to Coventry.

The present Cathedral was originally a Benedictine abbey founded in 1093 and incorporating earlier ecclesiastical buildings. It was dedicated to St Werburgh, the saintly daughter of Wulfere, ruler of Mercia, the Anglo-Saxon kingdom that included what is now Cheshire. The abbey played a very prominent part in the religious and secular life of a wide area centring upon Chester. It continued to do so until 1541 when following Henry VIII's Dissolution of the Monasteries, it became a cathedral. The former Roman Catholic abbot was appointed the new Anglican Dean.

Chester is known as a town of black and white buildings. These are eagerly photographed by tourists as examples of medieval architecture. Others take delight in pointing out that most of them are in fact Victorian creations and not medieval at all. These people are, however, only partly right. Several buildings in the main streets are indeed the work of well known Victorian architects, but the irony is that many of them are only Victorian *(continued on page 93)*

11

CHESTER

Chester

Roman amphitheatre   **NGR SJ 408662**

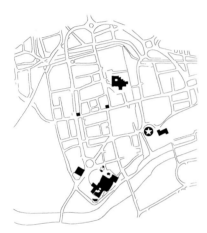

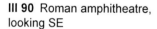

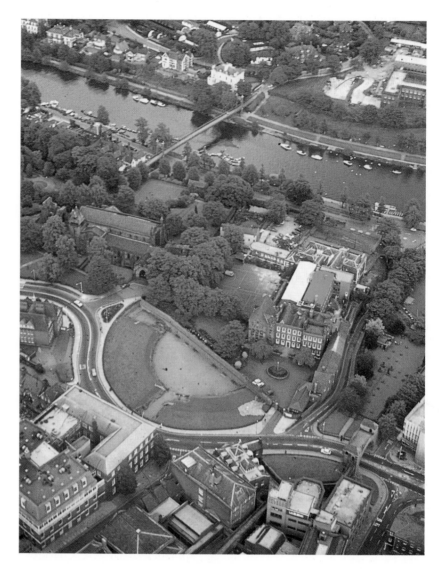

III 90 Roman amphitheatre, looking SE

Status
Scheduled Ancient Monument in the guardianship of English Heritage

References
Thompson 1976

Illustration 90, taken in June 1977, looks south-east over the amphitheatre and the Suspension Bridge over the River Dee.

The site was identified in 1929 by a member of the Chester Archaeological Society, this being confirmed when the Society carried out a trial excavation the following year. A public appeal was launched for funds to purchase the site and to explore it further. However, the outbreak of the Second World War rendered any further work impossible.

After the war, an agreement was reached between the Chester Archaeological Society, the City Council and the Ancient Monuments branch of the then Ministry of Works (now English Heritage) by which the Ministry of Works took it into guardianship under the terms of the Ancient Monuments Act. This meant that the site was protected by law and could only be investigated further with the approval of the Secretary of State.

Archaeological excavations were carried out on the northern half of the amphitheatre from 1960 under the direction of Hugh Thompson, then Curator of the Grosvenor Museum. It was discovered that the stone structure had been built about 100 over an earlier timber one probably erected in the late 70s. By about 120, it was evidently little used and had fallen into disrepair. It was re-

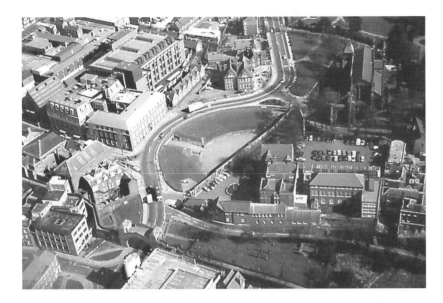

stored about 270, at which time the arena was floored with stone slabs, but was disused again by the end of the fourth century.

There was some residue from the funds collected in the 1930s for the purchase and exploration of the northern part of the amphitheatre. This was converted by the Charity Commissioners into a small trust fund (the St John's House Trust) which still exists to make grants towards the costs of archaeology in Chester and its environs.

While most people associate amphitheatres with gladiatorial contests and barbaric entertainments, those outside forts did have serious military uses. Among these were the demonstrating and practising of military manoeuvres and weapon training.

The southern part of the amphitheatre at Chester is still privately owned and is hidden beneath Dee House, whose basements will have destroyed parts of it. Illustration 91, taken in July 1978, looks east over the amphitheatre, with Dee House on its right. The City Walls may be seen at the bottom of the photograph, coming up to the twin-towered New Gate, just below the amphitheatre. The foundations of the Roman fortress's south-east angle tower may be seen where the medieval City Walls take a sharp turn east before resuming their course towards the north.

Chester *(continued from page 91)*

frontages to quite genuine medieval buildings. This is especially true of the area of the Rows along the city's four main streets. Recent research has demonstrated that the main structures of the buildings date from the late thirteenth century and were the balconied shops and dwellings of wealthy merchants. There is also much of considerable architectural interest in Chester, both inside and outside the City Walls, dating from the eighteenth and nineteenth centuries. The interest ranges, for example, from the magnificent Georgian Abbey Square to the lesser Georgian alleys and courts behind St Peter's Church, and from the exuberant Victorian woodwork of St Werburgh Street to the less important but hardly less restrained brickwork of Lumley Place.

Chester

Church of St John the Baptist   **NGR SJ 409661**

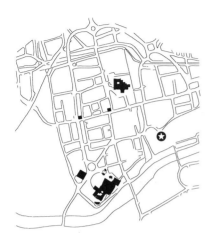

Ill 92 Church of St John the Baptist, looking NW

Illustration 92 was taken looking north-west in August 1981. It shows the nave and aisles of the Norman church together with the ruins of the original choir, chancel and eastern end of the nave, which was shortened in the sixteenth century.

The church stands on the site of an earlier one which is said to have been built by Ethelred, King of Mercia, about 689. St John's became a cathedral church in 1075 when Peter, the first Norman Bishop of Mercia, moved his seat from Lichfield to Chester. The Saxon church was replaced at that time with a new one on a very ambitious scale in the Romanesque style, with semi-circular arches on sturdy round pillars along the length of the nave.

Bishop Peter died in 1085 and was buried under the now-ruined choir outside the present east end. His successor moved his seat away from Chester to Coventry, and St John's consequently became a collegiate church, ie a church with a Dean and Chapter of Canons controlling a number of churches in its area, but without a bishop. Despite its reduced status, St John's remained a church of considerable importance. Unhappily, it was further reduced in status during the reign of Edward VI, when the nave was shortened by the building of a new east wall. This truncated the nave arcade, leaving several bays unroofed and now ruined in the open. The church was further disfigured in 1881 when the massive west tower collapsed; it has never been replaced.

Like most cathedral churches, St John's had a close, around which stood the houses of the bishop, the dean, the canons and other clergy. There were also in the vicinity the hospital of St Anne, the chapel of St James and the cell of an anchorite (now well known as the Hermitage).

The areas to the south and west of St John's (ie, to the left and above the church in the photograph) have a considerable archaeological potential. The presence of the Roman amphitheatre (seen at the top of the photograph), together with St John's seventh-century forerunner, suggests that the potential ranges from pagan Roman and early Christian times through the medieval period and, ultimately, to the present day.

References
Richards 1973, 103-10

Chester

The Cathedral   NGR SJ 406665

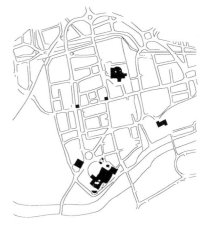

III 93 Chester Cathedral, looking SE

This aerial photograph, taken in July 1977, looks south-east over the Cathedral and Abbey Square, with the clock tower of the Town Hall towards the bottom right-hand corner. Abbey Square appears less spacious, perhaps, from the air than it does at ground level. What would otherwise have been a truly vast open space, extending the length of the great church and beyond, is partly taken up by the cloisters and the Refectory, as well as other less ancient buildings.

Immediately behind the Refectory may be seen what appears to be a long white marquee and a smaller tent. Between the marquee and the Cathedral's Chapter House, there is a circle of people dressed in white. A ceremony was evidently taking place or, more likely, a play was being performed, when the photograph was taken. As there does not seem to be an audience out in the open (perhaps they were in the marquee), it may be have been a rehearsal for a mystery play or pageant to be performed later.

The Cathedral was originally a Saxon church dedicated to St Werburgh, daughter of the king of Mercia (ie, the west midlands and Cheshire) and is possibly the site of an even earlier Romano-British church. After the Norman Conquest, Hugh Lupus, the first Norman Earl of Chester, brought a company of Benedictine monks from Normandy and founded an abbey here in 1093. He rebuilt the Saxon church on a grand scale, with what is now Abbey Square forming the greater part of the abbey's great court.

The Benedictine abbey of St Werburgh continued in existence until the Dissolution of the Monasteries in 1540 by King Henry VIII. It was then converted into a cathedral church with a dean and six canons, the former abbot, who had sought to please King Henry, becoming the new dean.

The old abbey buildings which lined the great court at the western end of the church have all but disappeared. Notable among those fragments that remain are the Abbey Gateway opposite the Town Hall and Little Abbey Gateway opposite the end of Hunter Street. There is also a chapel dedicated to St Thomas (not open to the public), within the basement of the Bishop's House at the head of Abbey Street. The fine houses that now line the north and west sides of Abbey Square are of various dates but all were built in the period from about 1750 to about 1830.

References
Burne 1958; 1962
Richards 1973, 93-101

Chester

The Old Dee Bridge and the weir   **NGR SJ 408657** (centre of photograph)

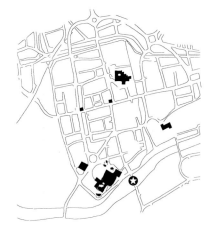

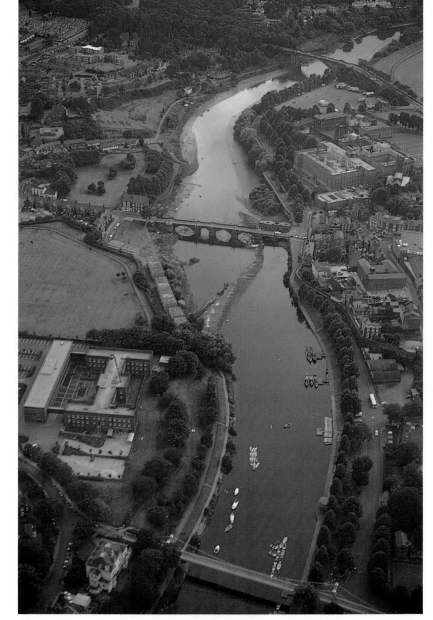

Ill 94 The Old Dee Bridge and the weir, looking SW

This photograph was taken in August 1980 and looks downstream, with the Old Dee Bridge in the centre. The suspension bridge can be seen at the very bottom of the picture and the Grosvenor Bridge in the distance. The former Western Command Headquarters building is on the left, and Chester Castle with County Hall on the right immediately beyond the Old Dee Bridge.

The Old Dee Bridge is on the line of the Roman road running from Chester *via* Aldford to Whitchurch and the south, and is probably sited near where a Roman bridge once stood.

A bridge at this point was mentioned in the Domesday Survey. It is thought that it was probably built of wood at that time. It is not certain when it was replaced with a stone bridge, but the present structure seems to have been in place by 1387 when King Richard II allowed the city authorities to use tolls obtained from river traffic, as well as other local taxes, for urgent repairs. It lay on an important route between Chester, Wales and the south, doubtless carrying much traffic and needing constant maintenance. It also seems to have been a defensible bridge, as there were two strong towers, one at each end. No trace of these now remains.

The weir, or causeway as it used to be called, was created by Hugh Lupus, nephew of William the Conqueror and first Norman Earl of Chester, who also created a number of fisheries in the deep water above it. He also built the first mills, at the north end of the Old Dee Bridge (on the right of the photograph) and it can be seen that the weir channels water to this point. At first, there was just one mill, but in 1093, the Earl granted space for a mill to the abbot of St Werburgh's. The abbot eventually also had another mill sited at the Bache, where there was a fast-flowing stream and a pool.

In time, several mills were built at the Old Dee Bridge and became quite famous as the Mills of Dee. They formed an important part of the inheritance of the Earls of Chester and were leased out to private persons for grinding corn and fulling cloth. The later mills were at the southern end of the weir, where the remnants of an old water wheel may still be seen near the salmon leap.

The citizens of Chester were required to bring their grain to one or other of the Chester mills, and there seems to have been considerable rivalry and friction between the various mill owners. Corn milling was a profitable business and the miller was allowed to retain a percentage of each sack of grain brought to his mill. The old song 'There was a jolly miller once lived on the River Dee' refers to the Dee mills. Well could the miller have been a rotund and jolly person without a care in the world: he made a good living.

The north bank of the Dee below County Hall and the Castle (just beyond the bridge, on the right in the photograph) was a part of Chester given over to skinning and tanning. It was not, then, the pleasant area that it is now, and it is thought-provoking that the cells of the gaol (part of the Castle) faced onto this area. What little ventilation the cells had would undoubtedly have admitted smoke from the fires and all manner of obnoxious odours to add to the sufferings of those incarcerated within.

Status
The Old Dee Bridge is a Grade II Listed Building

References
Driver 1971, 23, 54
Husain 1973, 39-40

12

CHESHIRE'S MERSEY SHORE

THE estuary of the River Mersey always seems to have been important, both as a route into the hinterland of north-west England and as a political frontier. The hillfort on Helsby Hill would have been a fine vantage point from which to observe any traffic passing along the river. Water levels would have been higher then and the shoreline nearer to the hill's sandstone cliffs. Bronze Age burial mounds and finds of flint tools in the region of Warrington suggest settlements and probably an important river crossing. A prehistoric route undoubtedly started in the Helsby-Frodsham area and followed Cheshire's central sandstone ridge to Beeston and places further south.

In Roman times, and presumably the late Iron Age as well, the estuary was the boundary between two tribes - the Brigantes of northern England and the Cornovii of the west midlands - and was watched over by a fortlet at Ince. Otherwise, there is as yet little direct evidence for Roman interest in the greater part of the estuary: the road between Chester and Roman Warrington (Wilderspool) was sited further inland, and most of the known Roman activity comes from the peninsula of Wirral, but overlooking the Dee rather than the Mersey. However, a collection of lead ingots has been found on the shore at Halton, possibly suggesting transhipment there.

In the Dark Ages the Mersey was again important as a frontier, between the kingdoms of Northumbria and Mercia. During these centuries, Cheshire was invaded by Danes from the north-east and Norsemen from their settlements in Ireland. A place-name ending in -by is a good indication of this Scandinavian incursion. They are known to have colonised parts of west Cheshire, including Chester itself, but their incursions into the Mersey estuary probably did not go beyond Helsby. That and Whitby, near Ellesmere Port, are the only place-names with the suffix -by east of Wirral.

The estuary was probably best known in the Middle Ages for the founding of Stanlow Abbey in 1172. Typical of a Cistercian foundation, it was sited in as inaccessible a place as possible on Stanlow Point. However, the buildings suffered a series of disasters by fire and flood, and in 1296 the monks left the area for a new foundation at Whalley in Lancashire.

Together with the River Irwell, the Mersey was improved for navigation during the eighteenth century. However, the silting of these rivers had always been a problem, and even now the extent of the silts is quite surprising when viewed from a an aircraft. Because of these difficulties of navigation, a system of canals was built. The St Helen's Canal, built in 1757, connected the south Lancashire coalfield with the Mersey and thereby with Liverpool. In 1765 the Bridgewater Canal connected collieries at Worsley, near Salford, with the Mersey estuary at Runcorn. Thus, south Lancashire coal was linked with Cheshire salt and so provided the basis for Cheshire's important chemical industry around Widnes, Runcorn, Northwich and Warrington. There was, however, a difficulty in that the route to the sea from Runcorn and Widnes was hazardous due to the navigable channels continually changing their position. This ultimately led to the construction of the Manchester Ship Canal, opened in 1894. It was probably this which most influenced the development of industry in the region and the rapid expansion of towns such Ellesmere Port and Runcorn. In 1881 the population of Ellesmere Port was 1,500, but by 1901 it had risen to 10,400. Since then the population of the area has been further reinforced by the oil and petrochemical industries which have come to Stanlow adjoining Ellesmere Port.

Ellesmere Port

Eighteenth-century canal basin   **NGR SJ 405773**

III 95 Ellesmere Port canal basin, looking E

In the eighteenth century canals were very important because of the ease and economy with which goods could be transported along them between one region and another, and from remote inland areas to outlet points on major rivers and along the coast.

It was proposed in 1793 that the rivers Dee, Severn and Mersey should be linked by a canal, with branch canals serving the west midlands, with their potteries, and industrial north-east Wales (the Llangollen branch). After some modifications, the scheme was put in hand and the 'Wirral line' of the Ellesmere Canal (later incorporated in the Shropshire Union Canal) was built between 1793 and 1795. It derived its name from the small Shropshire town of Ellesmere, and Ellesmere Port was simply the port at the end of the canal.

Taken in August 1983 and looking east, the photograph shows the basin and docks where the former Ellesmere Canal (seen coming in near the top right-hand corner) meets the Manchester Ship Canal (seen at the left of the picture). This elaborate eighteenth-century canal complex, which is now the Ellesmere Port Boat Museum, comprised large and small docks, a small dry dock, an upper and a lower basin, barge locks, a ship lock, several warehouses and stores, a blacksmith's forge and other workshops.

The early history of Ellesmere Port and its canal is closely associated with the great engineer Thomas Telford (1757-1834). He designed, among other things, a fine group of warehouses which stood on the island areas in the middle of the basin and spanned the narrow channels. Narrow canal boats entered these channels and stopped beneath the warehouses, enabling goods to be hoisted up into the storage areas above. Having been unloaded and perhaps taken on a new load, the narrow boats would proceed along the channels and emerge into the rear part of the basin from which they re-entered the canal. Unhappily, the great warehouses, which were considered to be buildings of Special Architectural or Historic Interest, were burned down some thirty years ago, and the remains were demolished for safety reasons.

The entrance to the canal complex from the Manchester Ship Canal is distinguished by having a small lighthouse. So far as is known, this is unique, being the only canal lighthouse in Britain.

References
Herson 1996

Stanlow

Twentieth-century oil refineries **SJ 442753** (centre of photograph)

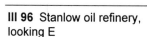

Ill 96 Stanlow oil refinery, looking E

The Stanlow area is a westward extension of a part of Cheshire that has long been associated with chemical industries. Well served first by the Shropshire Union Canal and then by the Manchester Ship Canal, it first attracted the oil industry in 1923, when Esso built a small refinery there. Since then, a number of other companies have become established at Stanlow, the largest, (at the time of writing) probably being Shell UK Ltd and its subsidiaries. The complex now stretches some 7 km (4½ miles) along the Mersey shore.

Relatively small tankers brought crude oil along the Manchester Ship Canal and discharged their cargoes at Stanlow, but with the advent of supertankers, the large Queen Elizabeth II Dock had to be built at Eastham, from where the oil was pumped along pipelines to Stanlow. Since then, a pipeline has been laid to Stanlow from a tanker terminal at Amlwch in Anglesey.

Runcorn

Road and railway bridges **NGR SJ 510835**

III 97 Runcorn-Widnes road and railway bridges, looking NW

The impressive steel arch of the road bridge connecting Runcorn and Widnes was opened in 1961 and is well illustrated by this photograph taken in April 1982, looking north-west. Runcorn and the Manchester Ship Canal are in the foreground with Widnes beyond, across the River Mersey. The massive stone and iron railway bridge can be seen behind the road bridge.

Runcorn was for centuries little more than a hamlet by-passed by the road from Chester to Warrington. Its outlet to the north was a ferry which had operated since the twelfth century.

The occurrence of salt in the Weaver Valley near Runcorn and the availability of coal transported from the northern coalfields by canal to Widnes soon led to the development of the chemical industry on both sides of the Mersey, and good transport across the river became essential. By 1803 there was a regular packet service between Runcorn and Liverpool, and by 1865 ferry boats were crossing the river to Widnes every five minutes. However, the ferry was not satisfactory, and several schemes for a road bridge were proposed. In 1748 James Brindley, the civil engineer, had proposed an aqueduct to carry the Bridgewater Canal across the river to Liverpool, and in 1818 Thomas Telford proposed a suspension bridge, very similar to his design for the Menai Bridge. However, the road transport problem was not resolved until the building of the well known transporter bridge, now demolished, early in the twentieth century. This was replaced by the present road bridge.

The railway bridge, which runs alongside the road bridge, is almost one hundred years older, having been completed in 1869. It has a footway running alongside the railway track. This, more than anything else, probably led to the decline of the medieval ferry which, however, managed to linger on until 1905 when it was finally discontinued.

References
Bott & Williams 1975, 47

101

Bibliography

Aberg, F A ed 1978 — Medieval moated sites. London: Council for British Archaeology. (CBA Res Rep **17**)

Barker, P & Higham, R 1988 — Hen Domen, Montgomery: a timber castle on the Welsh border. Excavations 1960-1988: a summary report. Oxford: Oxbow

Bott, O J P & Williams, S R 1975 — Man's imprint on Cheshire. Chester: Cheshire County Council

Bryant, A 1831 — Map of the County Palatine of Chester from actual survey in the years 1829, 1830 & 1831. London: Bryant

Bu'lock, J D 1972 — Pre-Conquest Cheshire: 383-1066. Chester: Cheshire Community Council. (History of Cheshire **3**)

Burdett, P P 1777 — A survey of the County Palatine of Chester. (Hist Soc Lancashire Cheshire Occas Ser **1**, 1974)

Burne, R V H 1958 — Chester Cathedral. London: SPCK

Burne, R V H 1962 — The monks of Chester. London: SPCK

Carrington, P ed 1994 — The English Heritage Book of Chester. London: Batsford

Davey, P J & Williams, S R 1975 — Ince Manor. *Cheshire Archaeol Bull* **3**, 24-8

Dodgson, J McN 1971 — The place-names of Cheshire, part **3**: the place-names of Nantwich Hundred and Eddisbury Hundred. Cambridge U P for English Place-Name Society. (English Place-Name Soc Vol **46**)

Dodgson, J McN 1972 — The place-names of Cheshire, part **4**: the place-names of Broxton Hundred and Wirral Hundred. Cambridge U P for English Place-Name Society. (English Place-Name Soc Vol **47**)

Driver, J T 1971 — Cheshire in the later Middle Ages. Chester: Cheshire Community Council. (History of Cheshire **6**)

Ellis, P ed 1993 — Beeston Castle, Cheshire: excavations by Laurence Keen & Peter Hough, 1968-85. London: English Heritage. (Archaeol Rep **23**)

Forde-Johnston, J 1976 — Hillforts of the Iron Age in England and Wales: a survey of the surface evidence. Liverpool U P

Frere, S S 1987 — Britannia: a history of Roman Britain. Ed 3. London: Routledge

Frere, S S & St Joseph, J K 1983 — Roman Britain from the air. Cambridge U P

Harris, B E & Thacker, A T eds 1987 — A history of the County of Chester **1**. London: Oxford U P for University of London Institute of Historical Research. (Victoria History of the Counties of England)

Herson, J 1996	Canals, railways and the demise of the port of Chester. *In:* Carrington, P ed. 'Where Deva spreads her wizard stream'. Trade and the port of Chester: papers from a seminar held at Chester, November 1995. Chester City Council. (Chester Archaeology Occas Pap **3**), 75-89
Hoskins, W G 1979	The making of the English landscape. Harmondsworth: Penguin
Hough, P 1982	Beeston Castle. *Cheshire Archaeol Bull* **8**, 22-30
Husain, B M C 1973	Cheshire under the Norman Earls. Chester: Cheshire Community Council. (History of Cheshire **4**)
Jones, G D B 1991	Farndon: an archaeological opportunity. *Manchester Archaeol Bull* **6**, 75-7
Laing, L & Laing J [1985]	The Dark Ages of West Cheshire. Chester: Cheshire County Council. (Cheshire Planning Monogr Ser **6**)
Lloyd, J E 1939	A history of Wales. Ed 3. London: Longmans Green & Co
Longley, D M T 1987	Later prehistory. *In:* Harris & Thacker eds, 103-14
Margary, I D 1957	Roman roads in Britain **2**. London: Phoenix
Mason, D J P 1982	Eaton by Tarporley 1980-81. *Cheshire Archaeol Bull* **8**, 49-52
Mason, D J P 1983	Eaton by Tarporley: excavations at the Roman villa. *Cheshire Archaeol Bull* **9**, 67-73
Mason, D J P 1988	The Roman site at Heronbridge, near Chester, Cheshire: aspects of civilian settlement in the vicinity of legionary fortresses in Britain and beyond. *Archaeol J* **145**, 123-57
North-West Civic Trust 1983	The treasures of Cheshire. Manchester: North-West Civic Trust
Ormerod, G 1882	History of the County Palatine and City of Chester. Ed 2 rev T Helsby. 3 vols. London: Routledge
Palin, W 1845	Cheshire farming. A report on the agriculture of Cheshire. London: Simpkin & Marshall/ Chester: Seacome & Prichard
Petch, D F 1975	Excavations in Eaton Road, Eccleston, Chester, 1972. *J Chester Archaeol Soc* **58**, 15-39
Petch, D F 1987	The Roman period. *In:* Harris & Thacker eds, 115-236
Richards, R 1973	Old Cheshire churches. Rev ed. Manchester: Moreton
Soulsby, I 1983	The towns of medieval Wales. Chichester: Phillimore

Sylvester, D & Nulty, G eds 1958 — Historical atlas of Cheshire. Chester: Cheshire Community Council

Taylor, A J 1974 — The king's works in Wales: 1277-1330. London: HMSO

Thacker, A T 1987 — Anglo-Saxon Cheshire. *In:* Harris & Thacker eds, 237-92

Thompson, F H 1976 — The excavation of the Roman amphitheatre at Chester. *Archaeologia* **105**, 127-39

Varley, W J 1950 — Excavations of the Castle Ditch, Eddisbury, 1935-8. *Trans Hist Soc Lancashire Cheshire* **102**, 1-68

Varley, W J *et al* 1940 — Prehistoric Cheshire. Chester: Cheshire Community Council

Waddelove, A C & Waddelove, E 1983 — Watling Street south of Chester. *J Chester Archaeol Soc* **66**, 13-22

Williams, S R 1978/9 — Aerial archaeology in Cheshire 2. *Cheshire Archaeol Bull* **6**, 12-18

Williams, S R 1984 — Tatton Old Hall: the rediscovery of a house. *Cheshire History* **13**, 4-6

Williams, S R 1984/5 — Aerial archaeology in Cheshire during 1984. *Cheshire Archaeol Bull* **10**, 11-18